MW01715003

Math in Focus®

Singapore Math®
by Marshall Cavendish

Fact Fluency

Author
Genevieve Collura

Reviewer
Susan Resnick

Grade K

Marshall Cavendish Education

U.S. Distributor
Houghton Mifflin Harcourt.
The Learning Company™

Published by Marshall Cavendish Education
Times Centre, 1 New Industrial Road, Singapore 536196
Customer Service Hotline: (65) 6213 9688
US Office Tel: (1-914) 332 8888 | Fax: (1-914) 332 8882
E-mail: cs@mceducation.com
Website: www.mceducation.com

Distributed by
Houghton Mifflin Harcourt
125 High Street
Boston, MA 02110
Tel: 617-351-5000
Website: www.hmhco.com/programs/math-in-focus

First published 2020

ISBN 978-0-358-10513-8

Printed in China

2 3 4 5 6 7 8 1401 25 24 23 22 21 20
4500799759 B C D E F

Contents

Preface

This book is part of your **Math in Focus®** program.
Each practice in **Math in Focus®** ***Fact Fluency*** can be completed in about ten minutes.
This is what you will do in this book.

- Practice what you learn in **Fact Builder** to help you remember math facts.
- Use different ways to solve problems in **Fact Strategy Practice**.
- Use math facts in **Apply and Build Knowledge** to solve real-world problems.
- Make new mathematical thinking in **Writing about Math**.
- Prepare for future learning with harder problems in **Challenge Questions**.

A scissors icon ✂ accompanies some practices. When you see the ✂ icon, cut and paste pictures found on pages 137 and 139 to complete the practice.

For Teachers and Parents

Math in Focus® ***Fact Fluency*** targets two critical elements of mathematical learning—conceptual understanding and fluency. Some activities focus on the understanding of grade-level skills and conceptual standards, while others focus on helping students achieve fluency expectations.

Mathematics Standards and Practices

Activities in **Math in Focus®** ***Fact Fluency*** align to the Common Core State Standards for Mathematics. At Grade K, these are:

Counting and Cardinality

- Know number names and the count sequence.
- Count to tell the number of objects.
- Compare numbers.

Operations and Algebraic Thinking

- Understand addition as putting together and adding to.
- Understand subtraction as taking apart and taking from.

Number and Operations in Base Ten

- Work with numbers 11–19 to gain foundations for place value.

Mathematical Practices

MP1. Make sense of problems and persevere in solving them.
MP6. Attend to precision.
MP7. Look for and make use of structure.
MP8. Look for and express regularity in repeated reasoning.

An Emphasis on Instruction

Students can be expected to complete each practice in **Math in Focus®** ***Fact Fluency*** in approximately ten minutes, making the practices useful as morning work, class openers, math center or station activities, and as homework.

Instructional Support

An Answer Key is available at the back of the book.

At the beginning of the year, students are likely to depend entirely on you for instructional support. Read directions aloud, and as you read, support student comprehension with physical actions, such as pointing, tracing, and clapping. Once you are confident that students are ready for greater independence, reduce guidance gradually.

Name: ________________________________ Date: ______________

Chapter 1

Fact Fluency
Numbers to 5

1a Working with 1 and 2

Color 1.

1

Color 2.

2

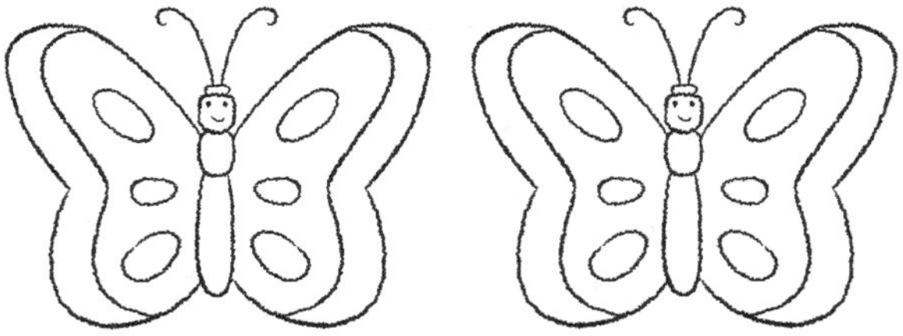

Match.

3

1b Working with 1 and 2

Trace. Clap. Cut. Paste.

1

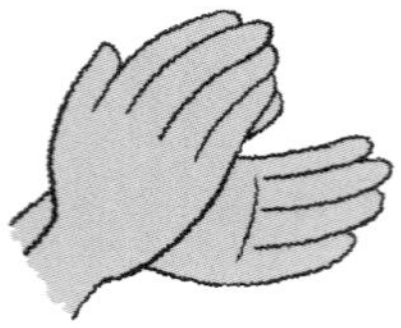

Trace. Color 2.

2

Count. Say. Clap. Trace.

3

4

1c Counting to 2

Color 2.

1 

Cut. Paste.

2

Count. Write.

3 How many  ?

4 How many  ?

5 How many  and  in all?

1d Counting to 3

Count. **Draw the same.** **Trace.**

1

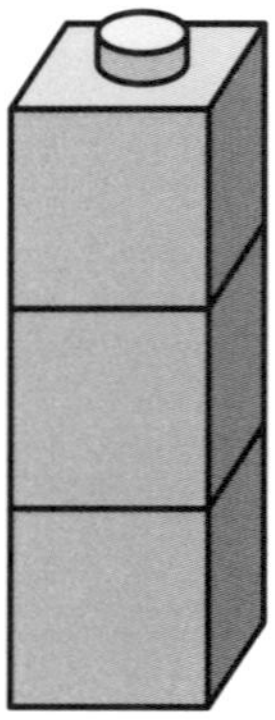

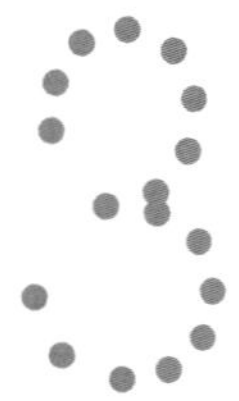

Count. Say. Write.

2

3

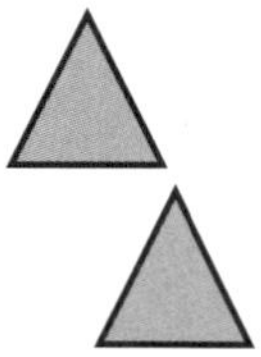

4

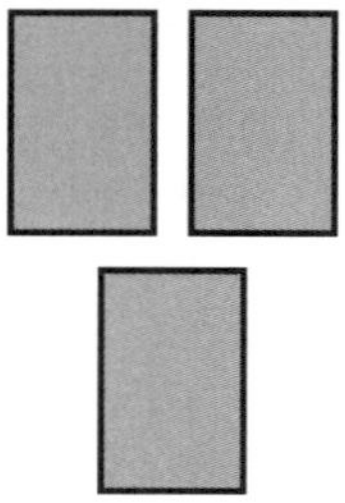

5

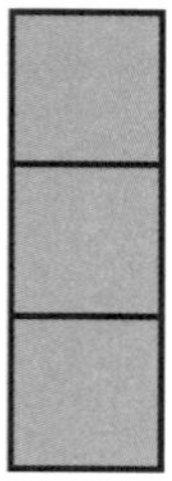

1e Counting to 4

Cut. Paste.

1

Count. Write.

2 How many  ?

3 How many  ?

Trace the correct number.

4 How many  and  in all?

1	2	3	4

1f Working with 4

Draw three ways to show 4 ♥.

1

2

3

1g Working with 5

✂ **Cut. Paste.**

1

Trace the correct number.

2 How many 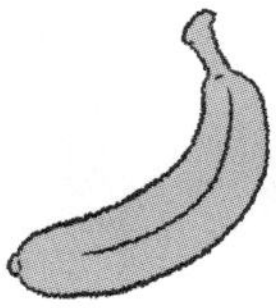 are there?

3 4 5

3 How many 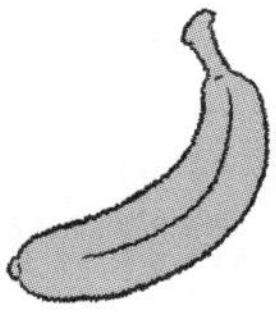 and  are there?

3 4 5

1h Working with 5

Count. Write.

1

2

3

4 **Color the group above that shows 4.**

5 **Circle the group above that shows 5.**

1i Working with 4 and 5

Color 4.

1

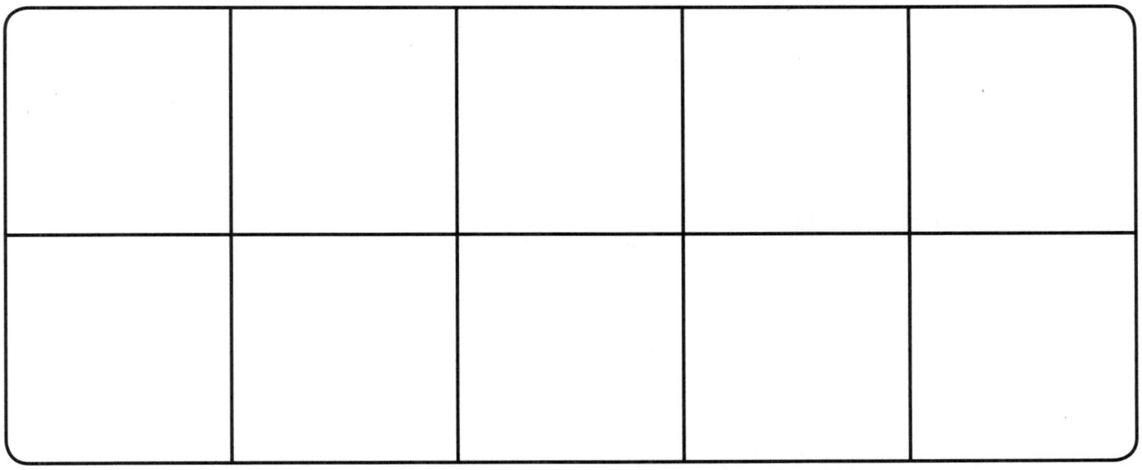

Color 5.

2

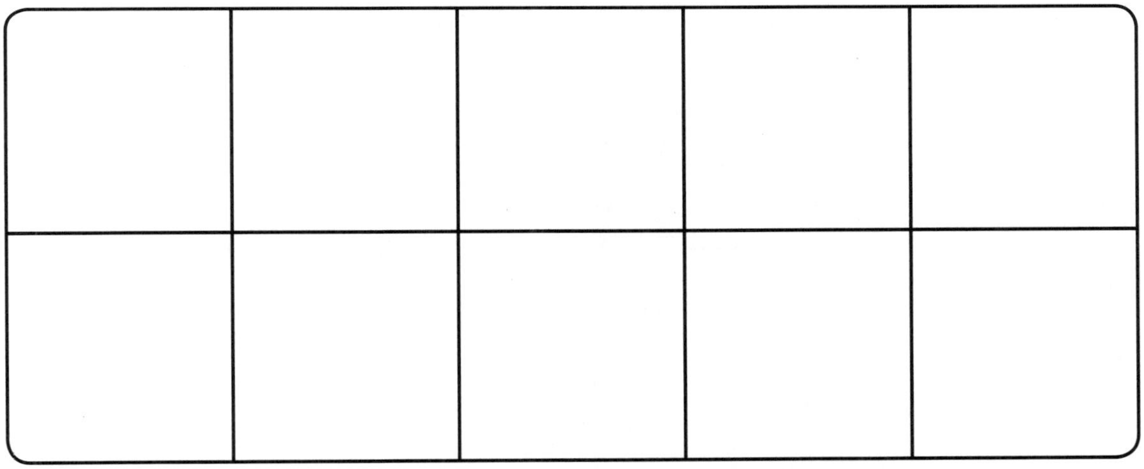

1j Numbers 1 to 5

Choose a number.

1 2 3 4 5

1 **My number:**

Draw three ways to show your number.

2

3

4

1k Numbers 1 to 5

Say. Clap. | **Draw.** | **Write.**

1 One 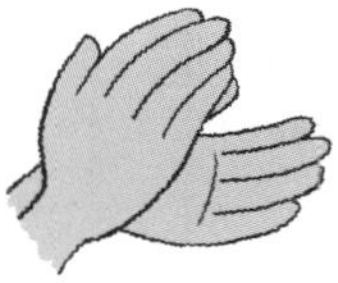

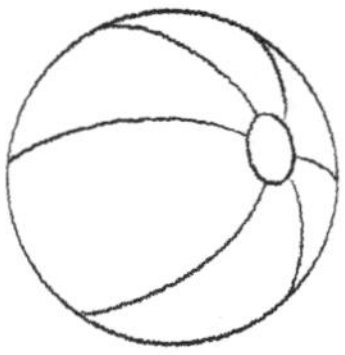

2 Two 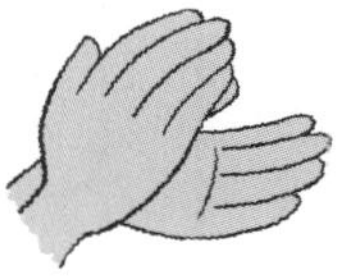

3 Three 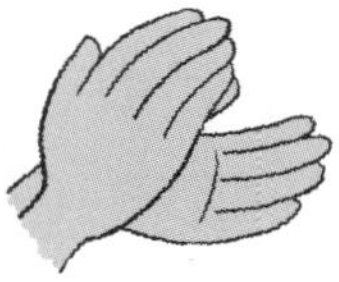

Say. Clap.	Draw.	Write.
4 Four 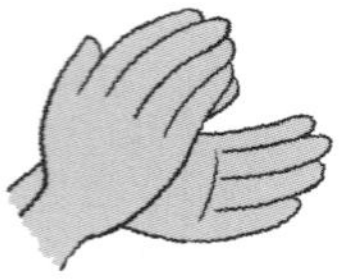		
5 Five 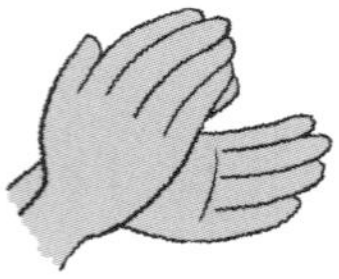		

Name: ____________________ Date: ____________

Fact Fluency
Numbers to 10

2a Working with 5

Match.

1

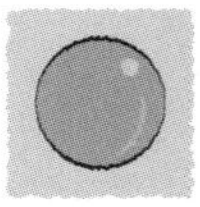 • • 4

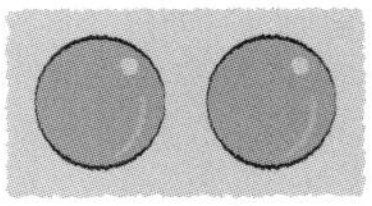 • • 1

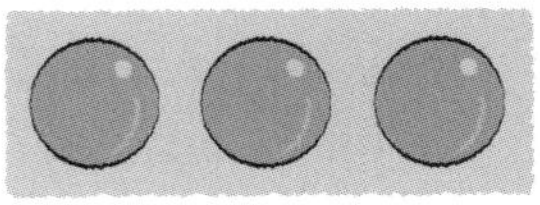 • • 2

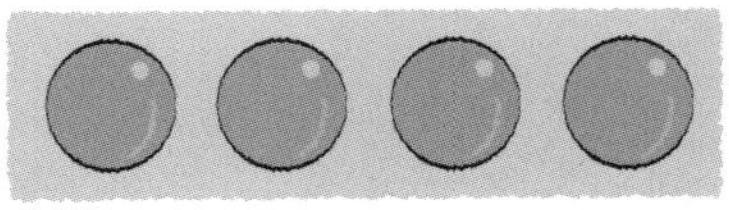 • • 5

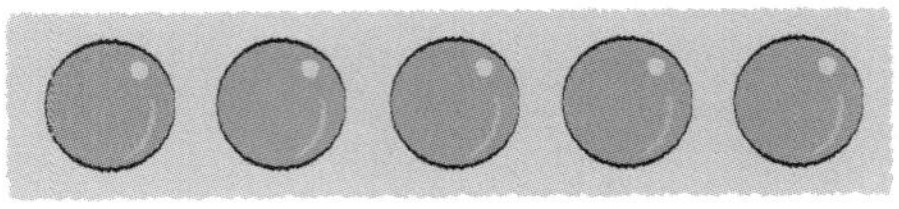 • • 3

2b Working with 6

Color the groups of 6 worms.

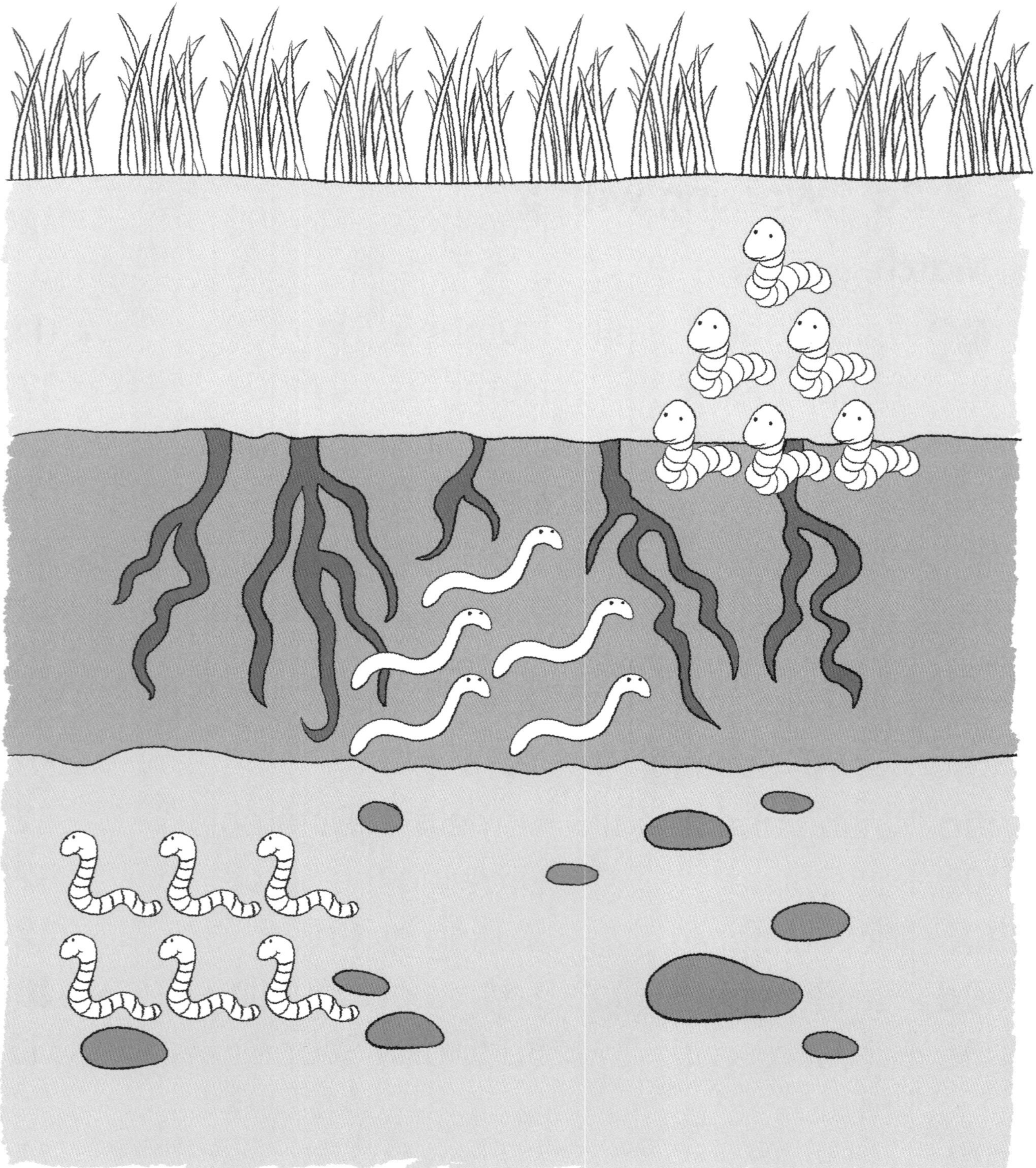

2c Working with 6

Count. Write.

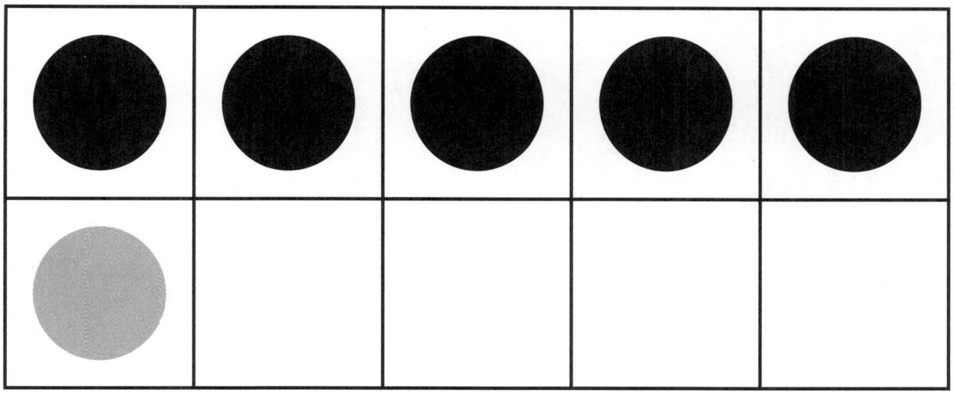

1 How many  ?

2 How many  ?

3 How many  and  in all?

2d Working with 7

Count. Trace.

1

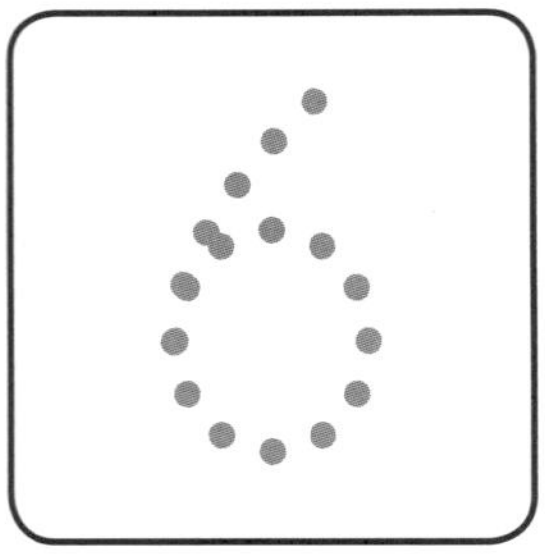

2

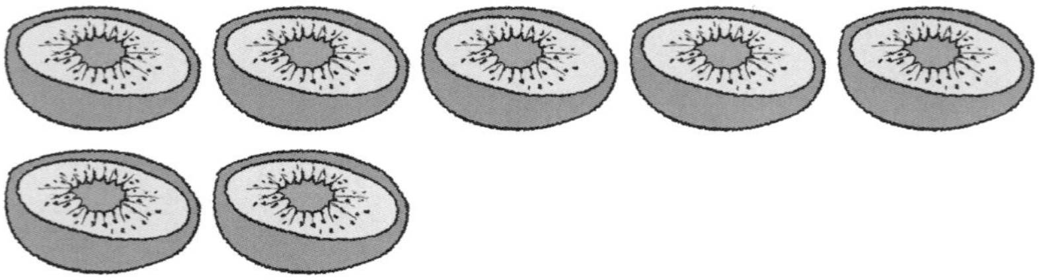

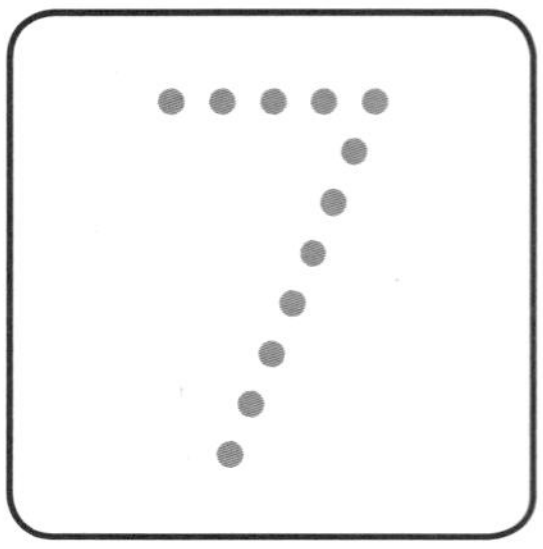

Color 7. Write.

3

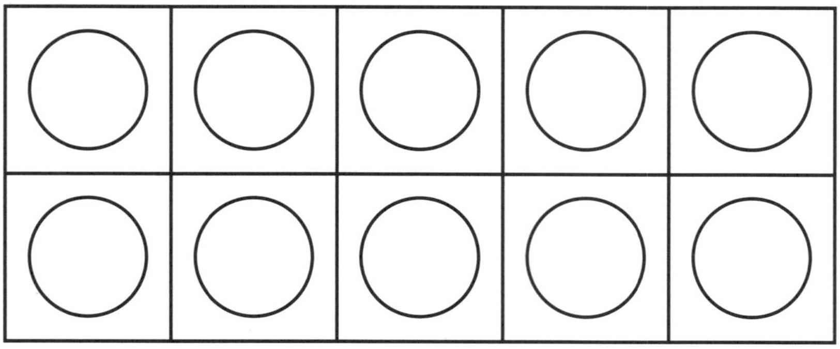

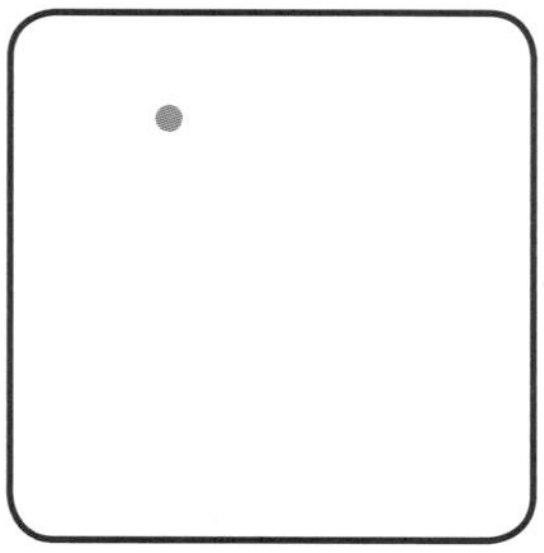

2e Working with 8

Color  **orange. Color** 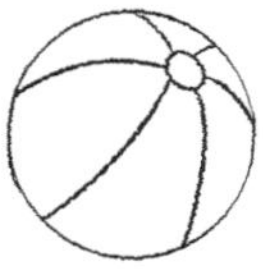 **brown.**

1

Count. Write.

2 How many  ?

3 How many 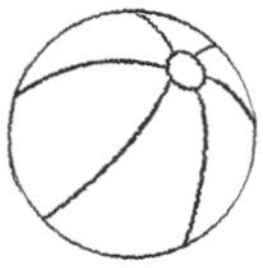 ?

Count. Trace.

4

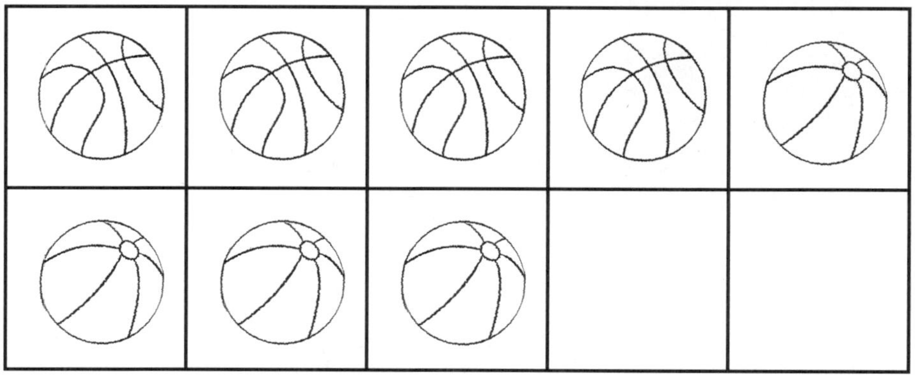

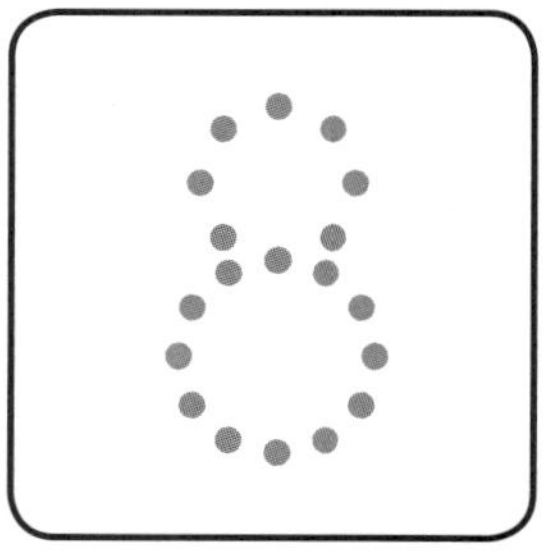

2f Numbers 1 to 10

Match.

1

 • • 8

 • • 6

 • • 5

 • • 9

 • • 7

2g Numbers 1 to 10

Color  **green. Color**  **red.**

1

Count. Write.

2 How many  ?

3 How many  ?

Count. Trace.

4

9

2h Numbers 1 to 10

Circle a number.

6 7 8 9 10

Draw three ways to show the number.

1

2

3

2i Numbers 1 to 10

	Say.	Clap.	Write.
	Six	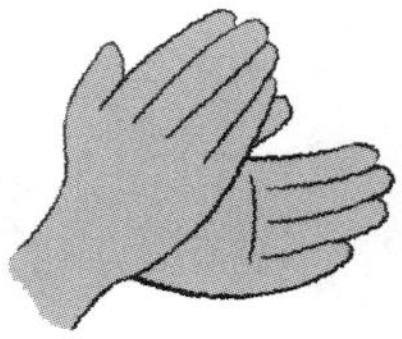	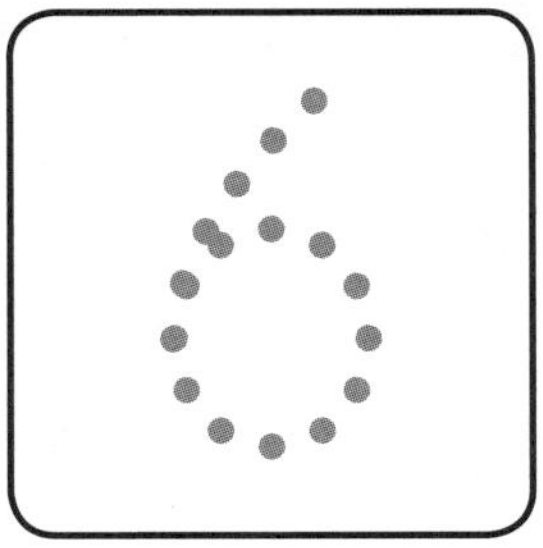
1	Seven	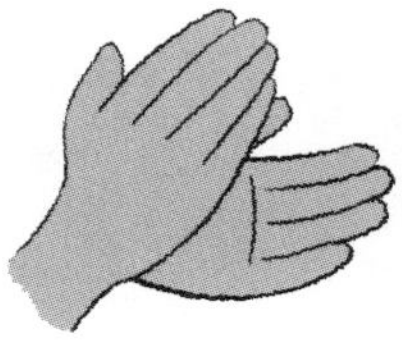	
2	Eight	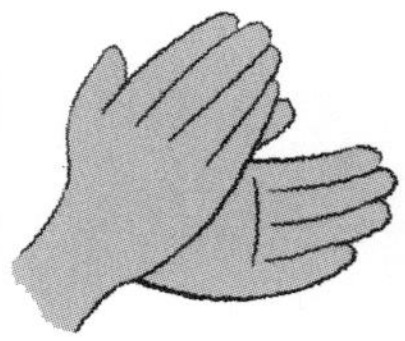	
3	Nine	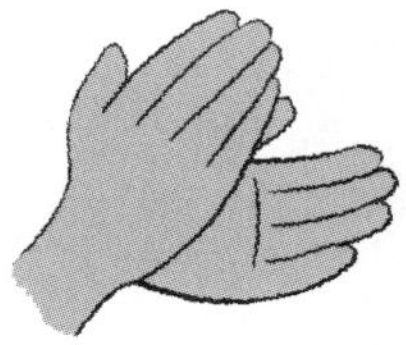	
4	Ten	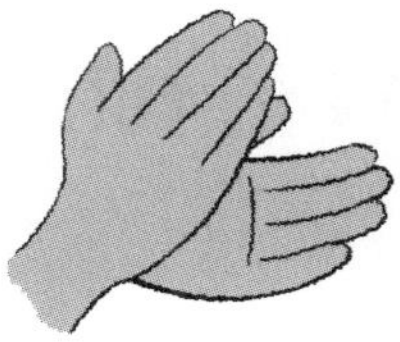	

2j Numbers 1 to 10

Use these pictures to draw any number to 10. Count. Write.

How many did you draw in all?

2k Number Facts to 5

Color some  **orange. Color some**  **purple.**

1 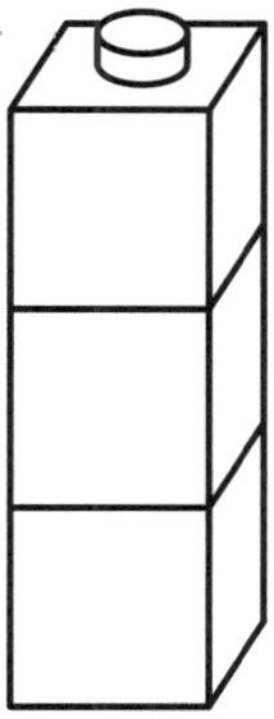

Count. Write.

2 How many  are orange?

3 How many  are purple?

4 How many  did you color in all?

2I Number Facts to 5

Count. Write.

1 How many  cross the finish line? ☐

2 How many  did **not** cross the finish line? ☐

3 How many  are there in all? ☐

2m Number Facts to 5

Count. Write.

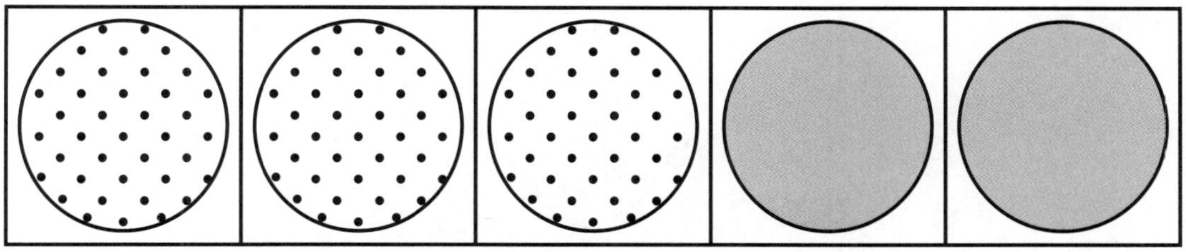

1. How many 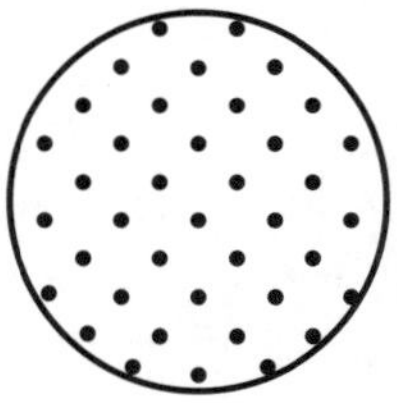 ?

2. How many  ?

3. How many 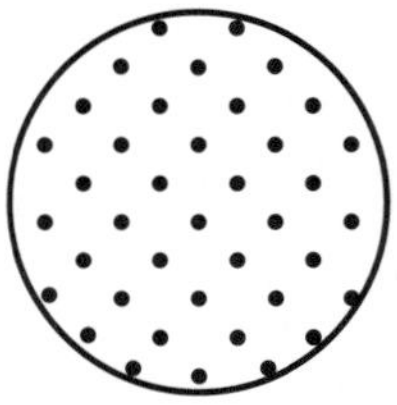 and  in all?

4. ________ and ________ make 5.

2n Number Facts to 5

Look at the picture.
Make a story.

Draw to tell your story.

2o Counting to 10

Count. Write.

1. How many  ?

2. How many  ?

3. How many  and  in all?

2p Counting to 10

Count. Write.

1 How many  ?

2 How many  ?

3 How many  and  in all?

4 ________ and ________ make ________.

Name: ____________________ Date: ____________

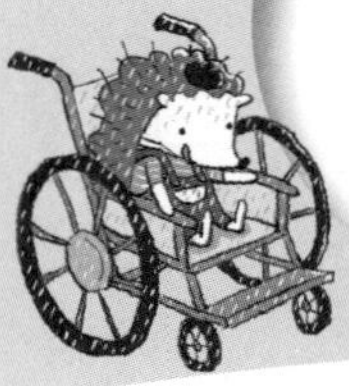

Chapter 3

Fact Fluency
Measurement

3a Comparing Length

Which is longer? Color.

1

Color all  **. Count. Write.**

2

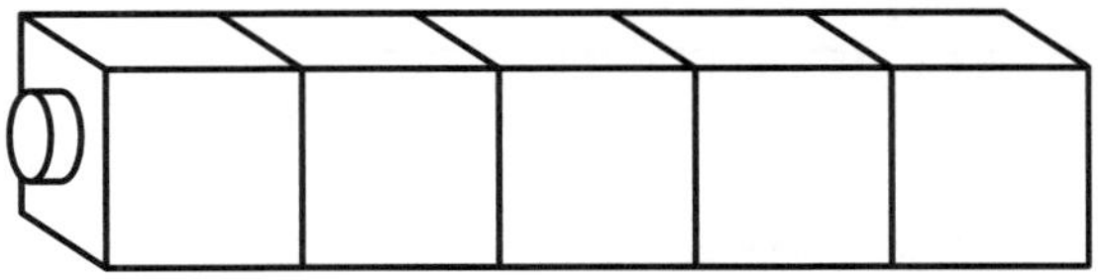

3b Comparing Length

Color the longer pencil.

1

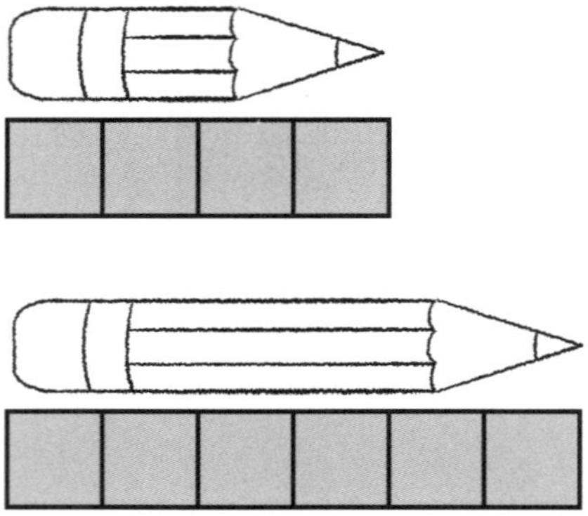

Count. Write.

How many ☐ long is it?

Color the shorter train.

2

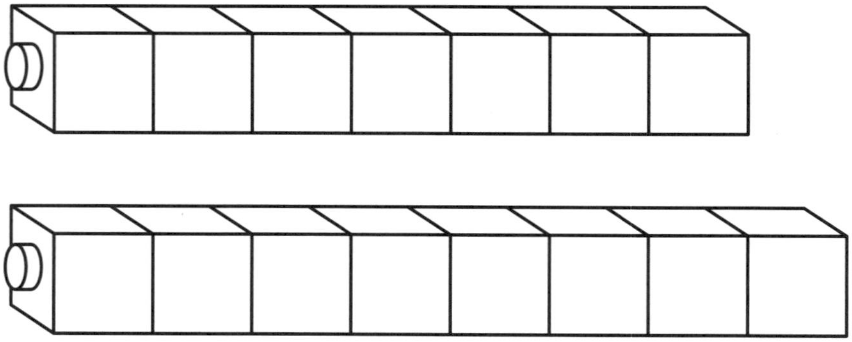

3c Comparing Length

Look at the train of ☐.

☐☐☐☐☐☐☐☐☐

Draw ☐ to make a shorter train.

1

Count. Write.

2 How many ☐ did you draw?

3d Comparing Height

Count. Write.

1

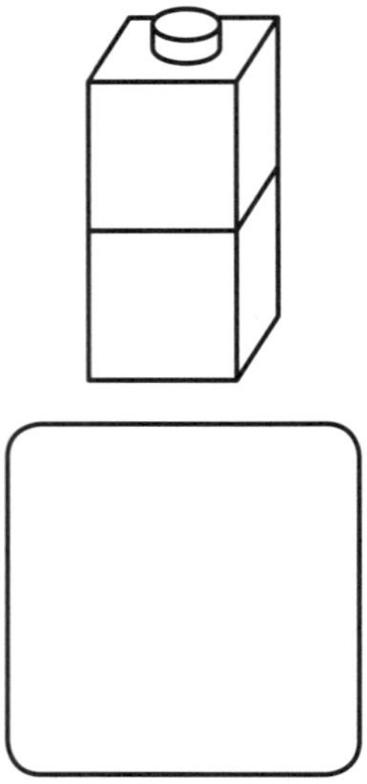

2

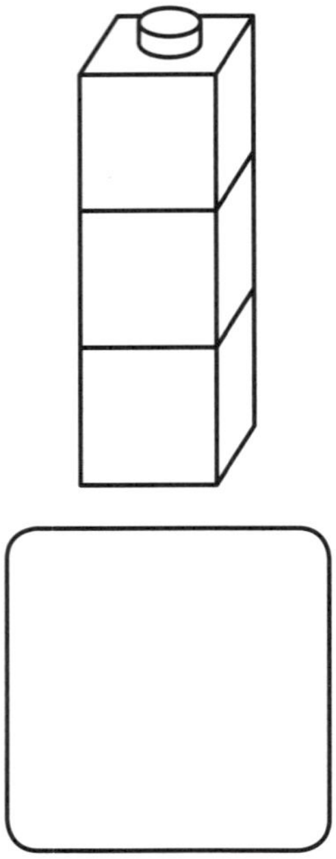

Circle the taller tower.

3

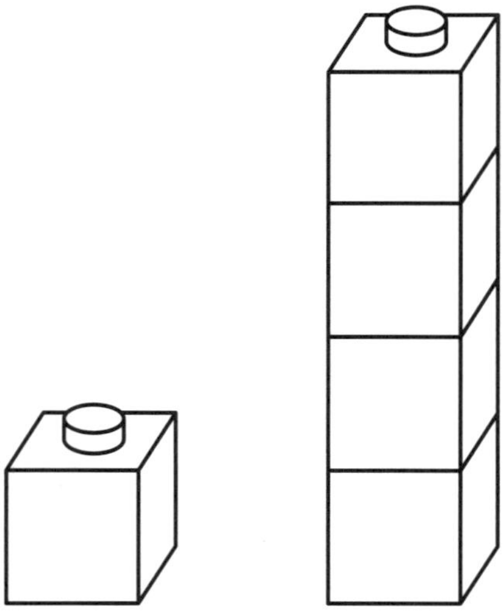

3e Comparing Height

Cut. Paste. Which is taller? Circle.

1

Count. Write.

2 How many  are there in all?

3f Comparing Weight

Count. Write.

1

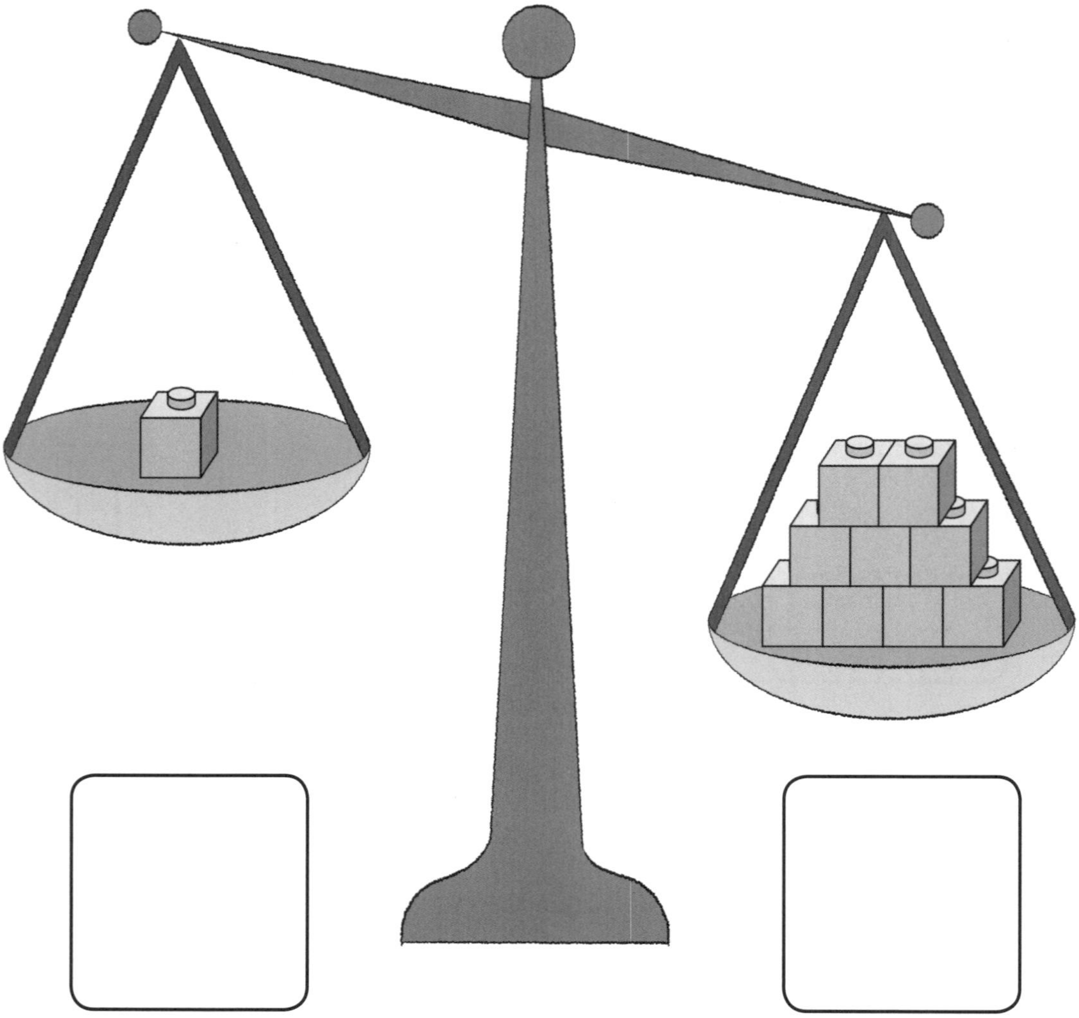

2 **Circle the lighter side on the** **.**
Tell your partner how you know.

3g How Tall Are They?

Color the shorter tower blue.
Color the taller tower yellow.

1

Count. Write.

2 How many  are there in all?

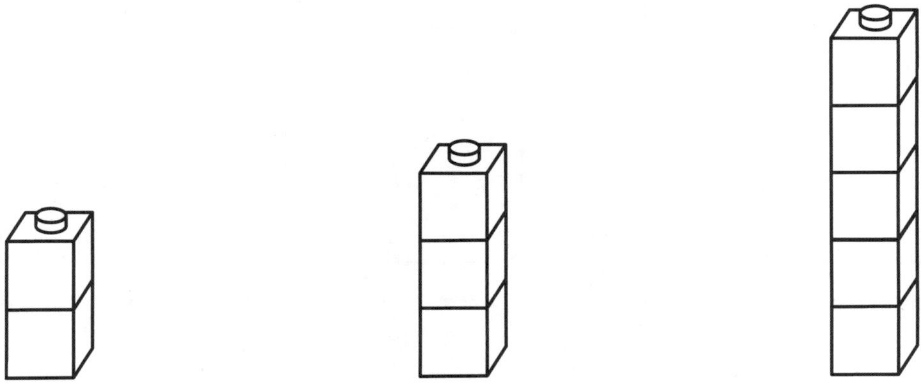

__________ and __________ make __________.

3h Comparing

Count. Write.

1 Set A Set B

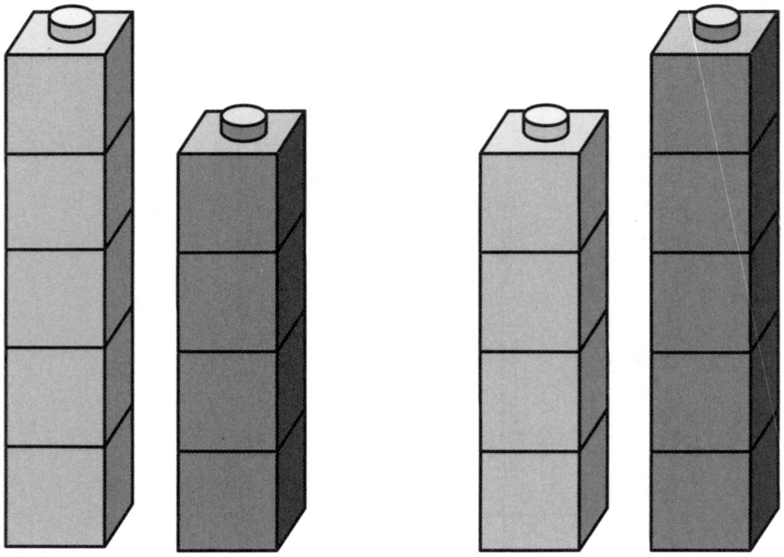

Color the correct box.

2 The number of  is the same / different.

3i What is the Length?

Count. Write.

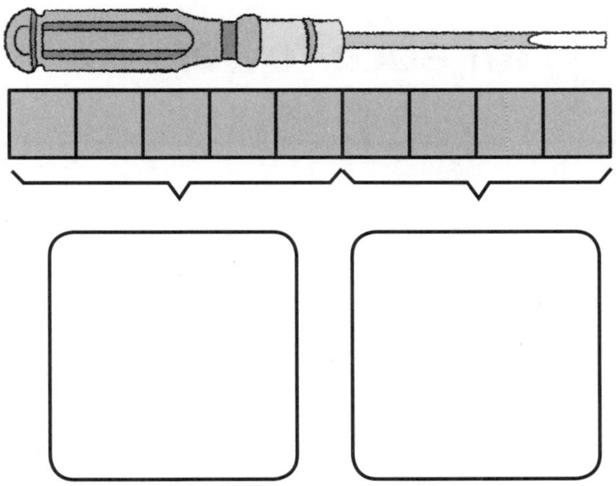

__________ and __________ make __________.

It is about __________ ▢ long.

3j Comparing Height

Draw a picture of two towers.

Use up to 5  **for each tower.**

1

2 **What story can you make?**
Use these words in your story:

more   less   taller   shorter   in all

Name: ______________________ Date: ____________

Fact Fluency
Compare Numbers to 10

4a Number Facts

Use your fingers on both hands.

1 Show 5.

2 Show one more number. Write.

3 Show another number. Write.

4b One More

✄ **Cut. Paste one more.**
Count. Write.

1
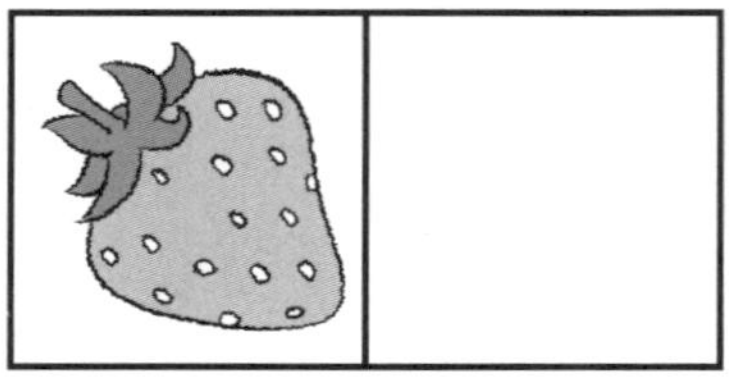

2

3

4

4c Fewer or More Within 10

Count the objects in each group. Write.
Circle the group that has more.

Example

5

4

1

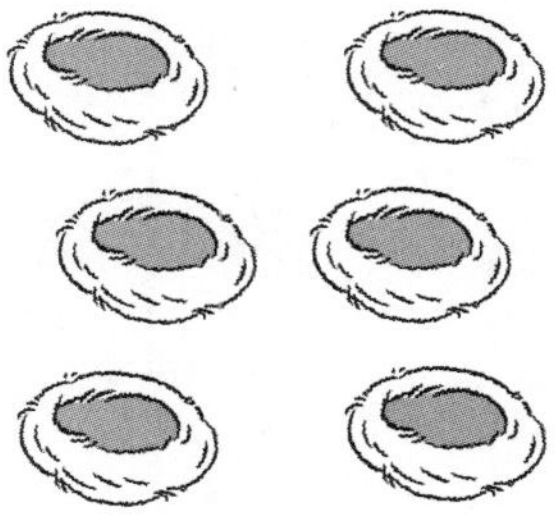

2

4d Fewer or More Within 10

Count the objects in each group. Write.
Color the group that has fewer.

Example

3 2

1

2

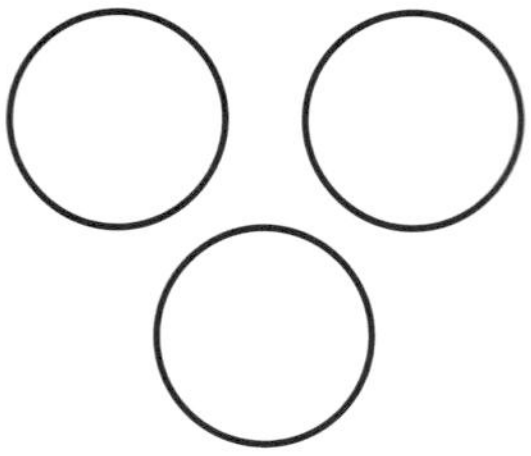

4e Fewer or More Within 10

Count the objects in each group. Write.
Circle the group that has fewer.

Example

4

2

1

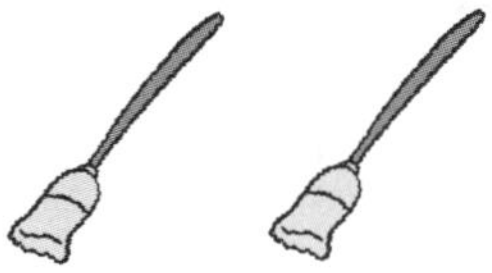

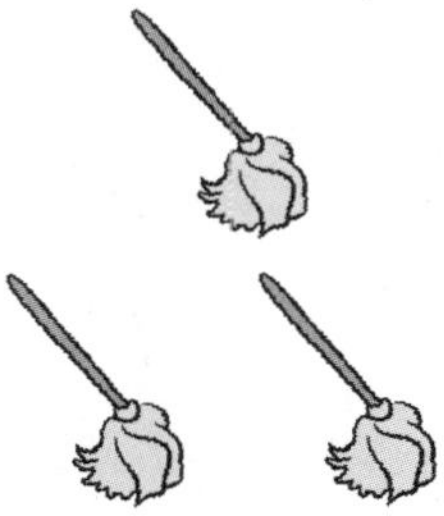

2

4f How Many More?

How many more  **do you need?**

Draw. Count. Write.

1 

How many more do you need? Draw. Count. Circle.

2 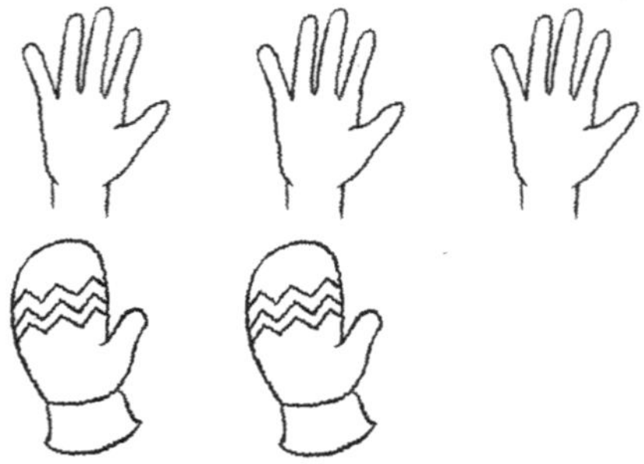

1 2

3 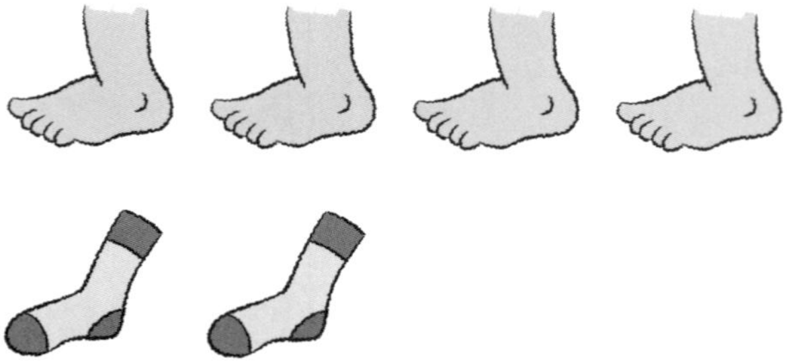

1 2

4g Counting to 10

Count. Write.

1

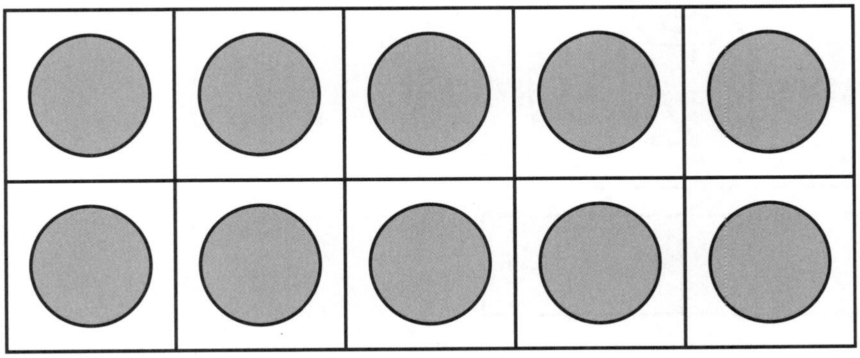

2

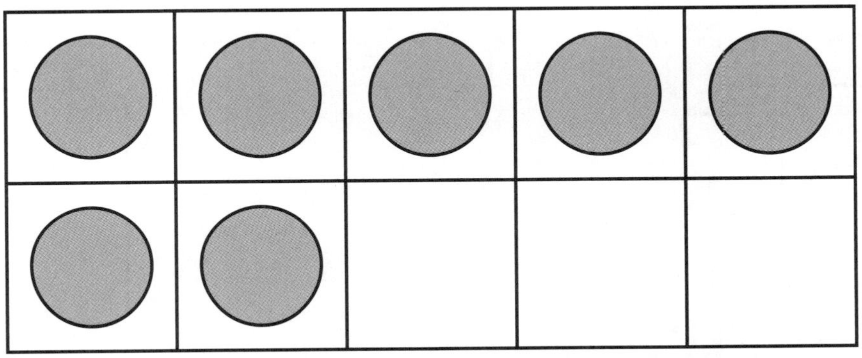

Draw more in .

Count. Write.

3 How many more did you draw?

4h How Many More?

Count. Write.

Which has more  **? Circle it.**

1 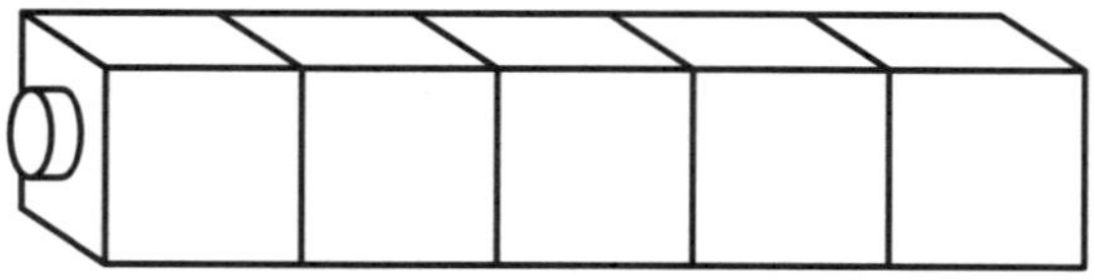

2 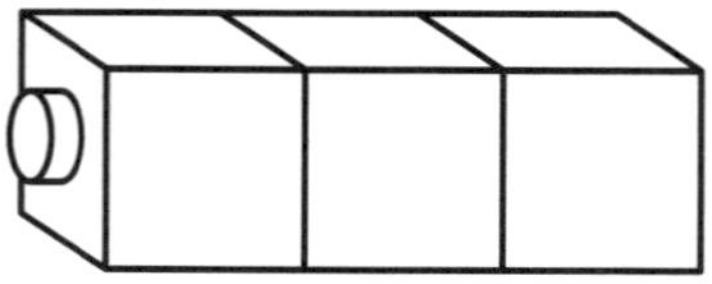

Count. Write.

3 How many  are there in 1 and 2 ?

4i Comparing Numbers to 10

Count. Write.

Which has more  ? Circle it.

1 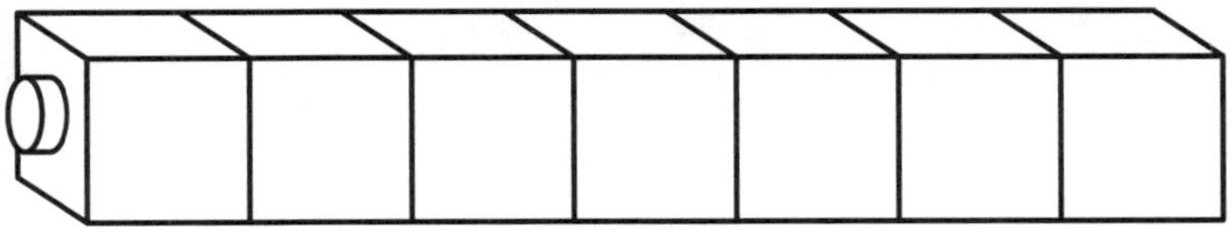

2 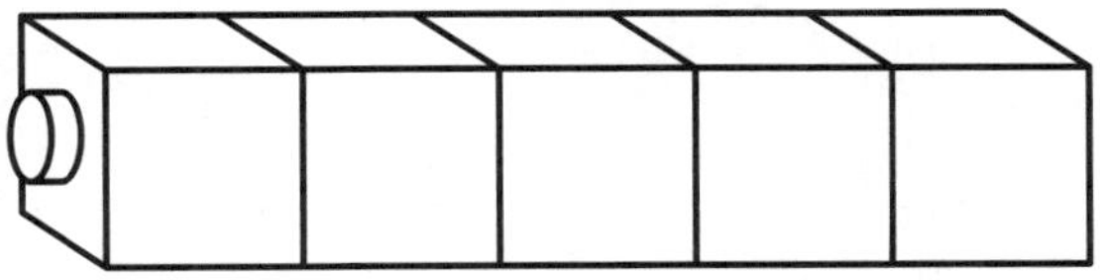

Mark an ✗ on  to make both trains the same.

Count. Write.

3 How many  have ✗ ?

4j Numbers to 10

Look at the picture.
Count. Write.

1 How many bears are there? ☐

Color the same number.

2

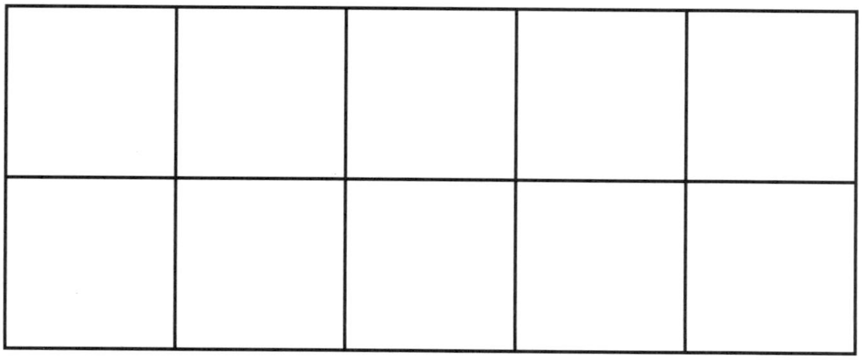

4k Numbers to 10

Look at the picture.
Make a story.

1 Tell your story to a partner.

Count. Write.

2 How many monkeys are there in all?

41 Counting to 10

Count. Write.

1 How many ?

2 How many ?

3 How many and in all?

4 ________ and ________ make ________.

4m Numbers to 10

Choose a number less than 10.
Draw a picture to show the number.

Share your picture with a partner.

BLANK

Name: ______________________ Date: ______________

Fact Fluency
Flat and Solid Shapes

5a Counting to 10

Count. Write.

1

______ and ______ make ______.

2

______ and ______ make ______.

5b Counting Sides

Count the sides. Write.

1

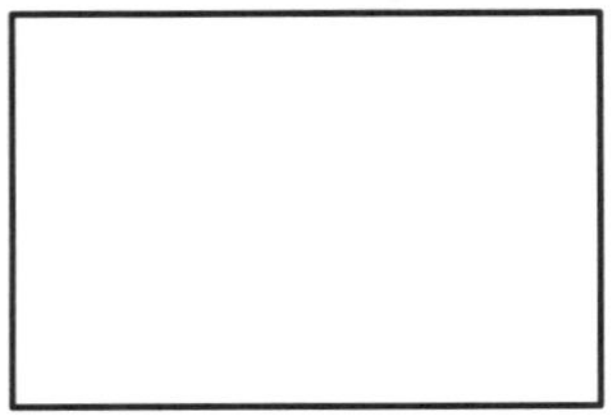

2

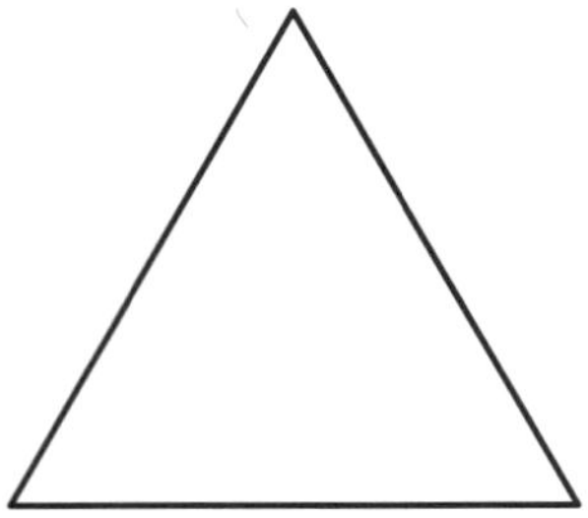

5c Counting Flat Faces

Count the flat faces. Write.

1

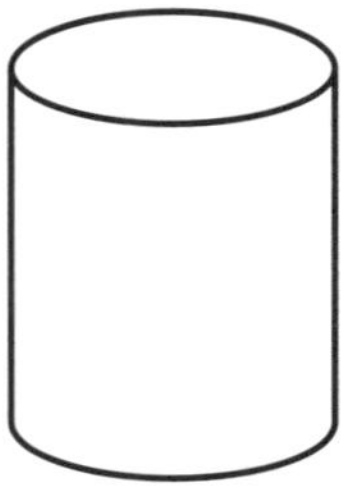

2

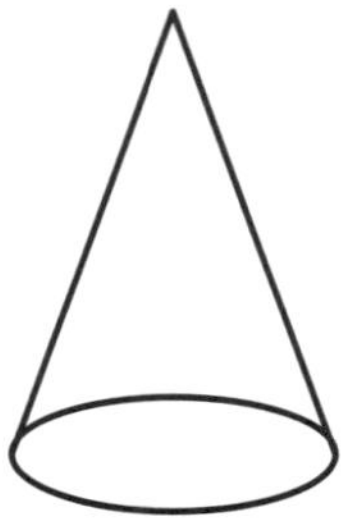

5d Knowing Solids

Color  red. Color 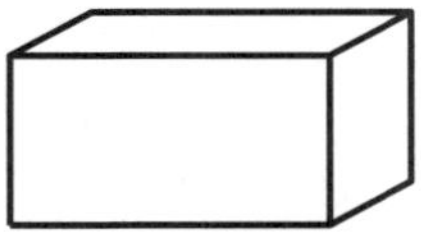 orange.

1

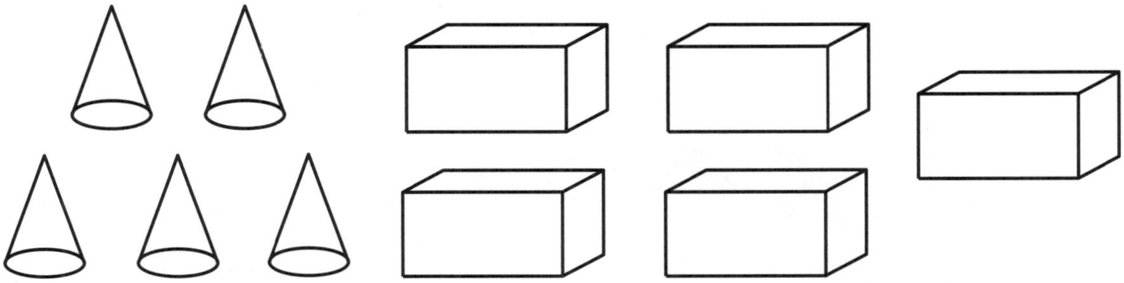

5e Counting Solids

Count the solids above. Write.

1 How many  ?

2 How many 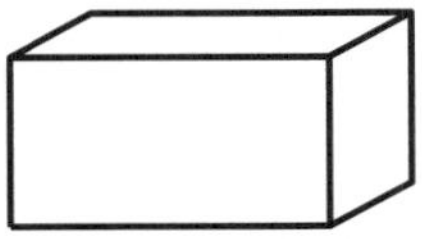 ?

3 How many  and 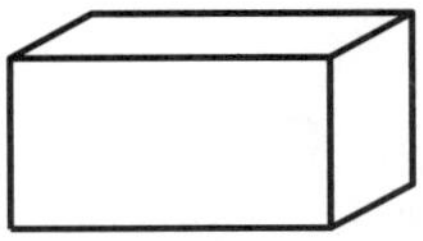 in all?

5f Knowing Positions

Count. Write.

1. How many  are **behind** the rocks? ☐

2. How many  are **next to** the tree? ☐

3. How many  and  are there in all? ☐

5g Knowing Positions

Count. Write.

1 How many  are **on** the table?

---

2 How many 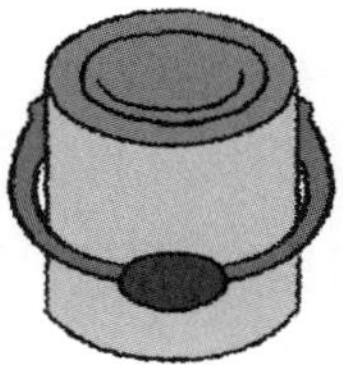 are **under** the table?

---

3 How many  and 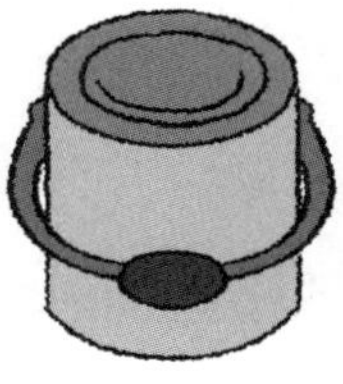 are there in all?

5h Knowing Positions

Count. Write.

1. How many  are **between** the trees?

2. How many  are **under** the trees?

3. How many  are there in all?

5i Counting Sides

Count the the sides. Write.

1

2

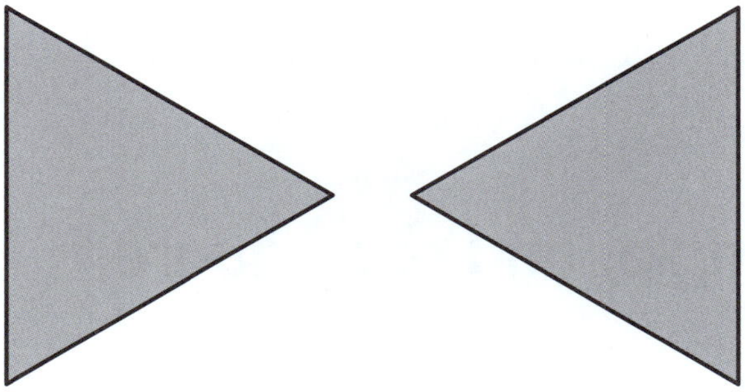

5j Counting Sides

Count the sides. Write.

1

2

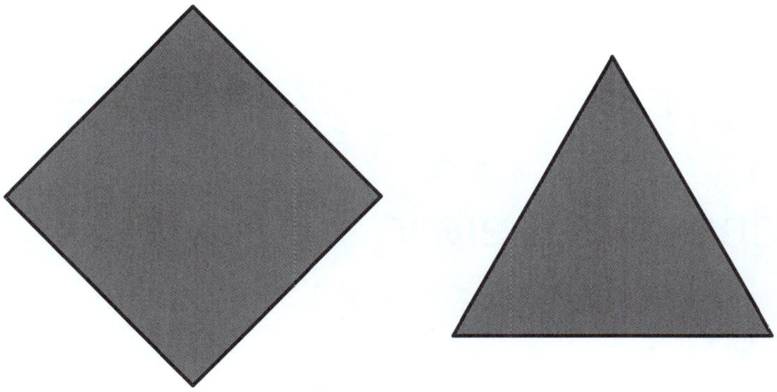

5k Flat Shapes

Draw two circles.

1

Draw a picture.
Use two circles, one triangle, and one square.

2

Count. Write.

3 How many shapes are there in 2?

5I Flat Shapes

Draw a picture.
Use two triangles and one circle.

1

Count. Write.

2 How many shapes are there in 1 ?

5m Same

Draw shapes in some ☐.

1

Draw the same shapes in another way.

2

Count. Write.

3 How many shapes did you draw in all? ☐

5n Counting and Arranging

Draw 2 of each ◯ and ☐.

1 Way 1:

2 Way 2:

Count. Write.

3 How many ◯ and ☐ did you draw each time?

5o Counting a Pattern

Count. Write.

How many 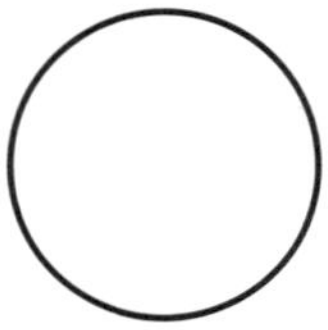 and 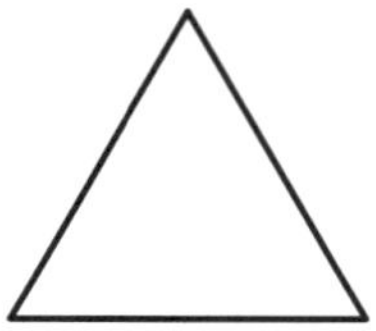 are there in all?

5p Shape Patterns

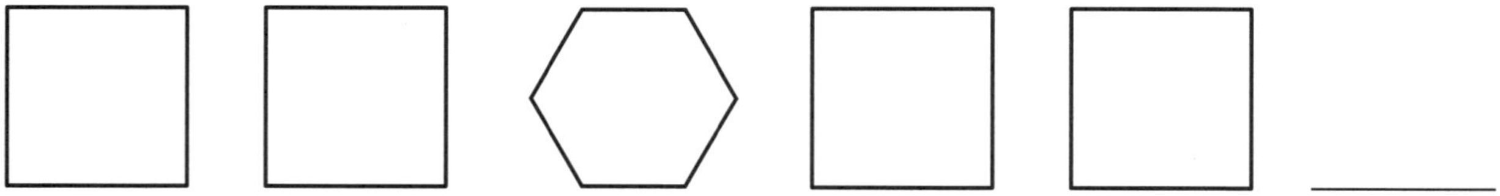

Draw.

1 What shape comes next?

Count. Write.

2 How many  ?

3 How many 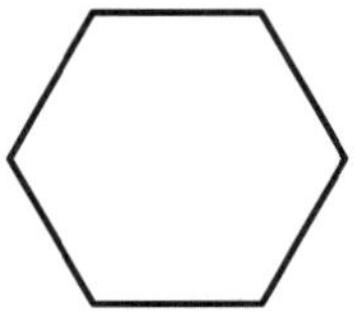 ?

4 How many shapes are there in all?

5q Counting a Pattern

Count. Write.

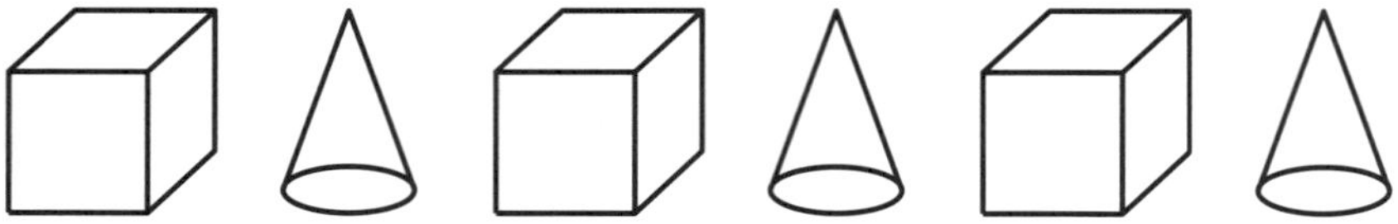

1. How many 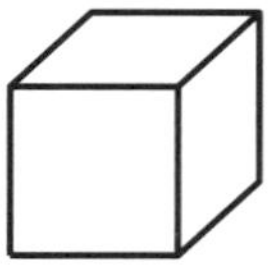 ?

2. How many  ?

3. How many 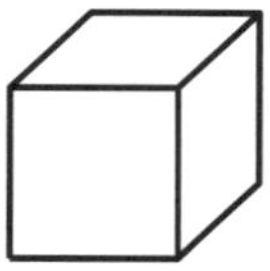 and 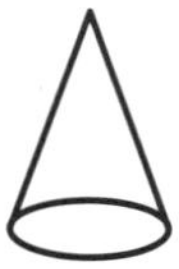 in all?

Name: ______________________ Date: ____________

Fact Fluency

Numbers to 20

6a Number Order from 1 to 5

Draw  **to show 1 to 5.**

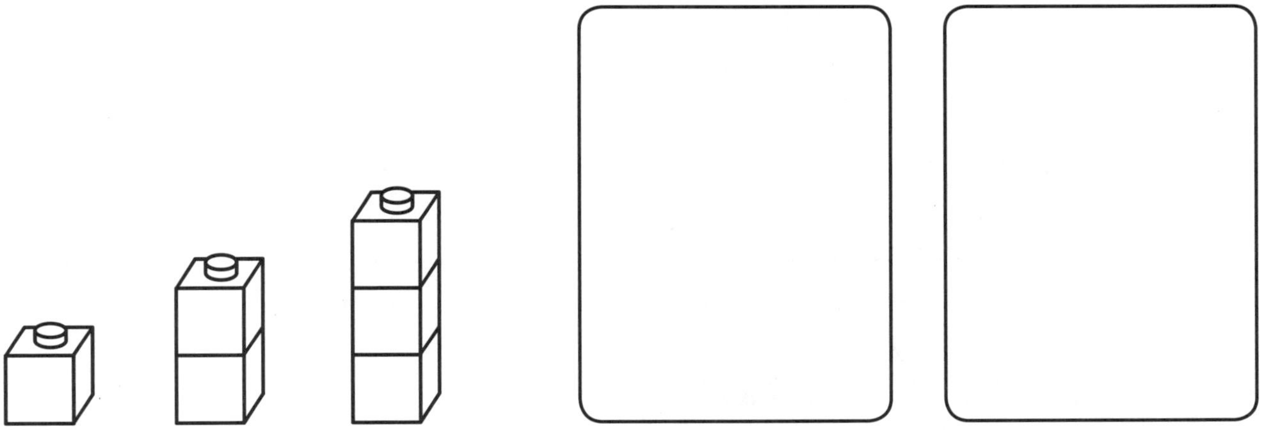

6b Numbers 11 to 13

Count. Write.

6c What is the Number?

Write.

1 Choose a number from 9 to 12.

Draw ✿ to show your number.

2

Draw 1 more △ than ✿.

3

Count. Write.

4 How many △ did you draw?

6d Numbers to 16

Count on. Write the number. Circle to make 10.

1 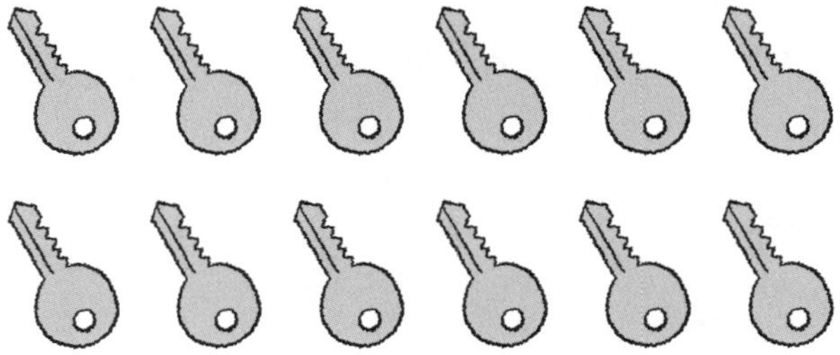

Count. Write.

2 How many  ?

---

3 How many  ?

---

4 10 and ________ make ________.

6e Numbers to 16

Count. Write.

1

Draw more to make 16 in all.

2

Count. Write.

3 How many did you draw?

6f Working with Numbers to 20

Circle to make a 10.

1

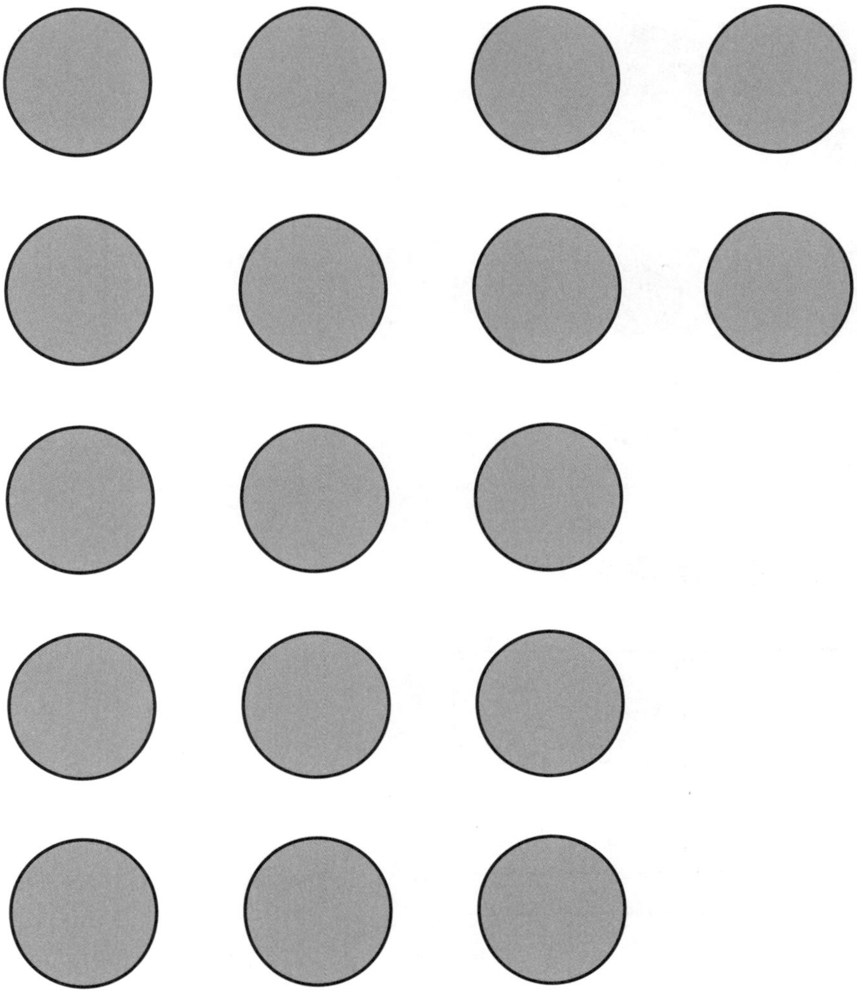

Count on. Circle the correct number.

2 How many  are there in all? **12** **17** **18**

6g Working with Numbers to 20

Count. Write.

1

Draw more 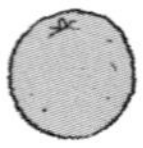 **to make 18.**

2

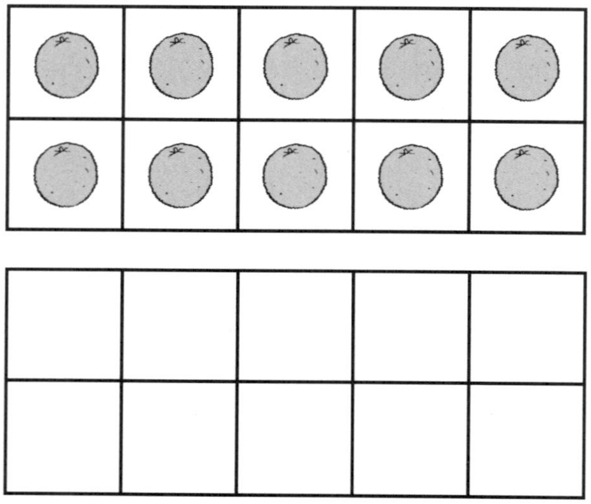

6h Counting On and Counting Back

Which numbers are missing?
Choose from the box below.

14 9 11
18 15 17

1. 8, ___, 10, ___, 12

2. 12, 13, 14, ___, 16

3. 20, 19, ___, 17, 16

4. ___, 16, 15, ___, 13

6i Counting On from 10

Count. Say. Write.

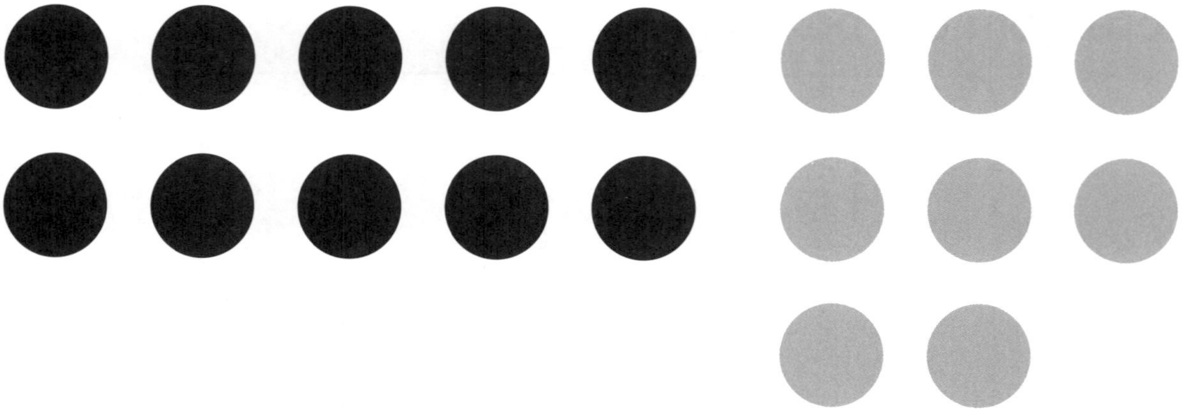

1. How many ?

2. How many ?

3. How many and in all?

4. ______ and ______ make ______.

6j Counting On from 10

Count. Say. Write.

1 How many  ?

2 How many  ?

3 How many  and  in all?

6k What is the Number?

Ask a partner to circle a number.

11 12 13 14 15

16 17 18 19 20

1 **Write the number.**

Draw to show the number.

2

6I Working with Numbers to 20

1 Draw 19 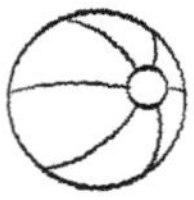. Circle 10.

Count. Write.

2 How many 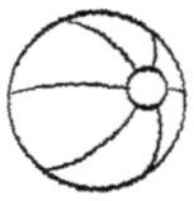 are **not** circled? ☐

3 ________ is ________ and ________.

BLANK

Name: ____________________ Date: ____________

Fact Fluency
Addition

7a Number Facts to 5

Use 2 colors to show 5. Count. Write.

1

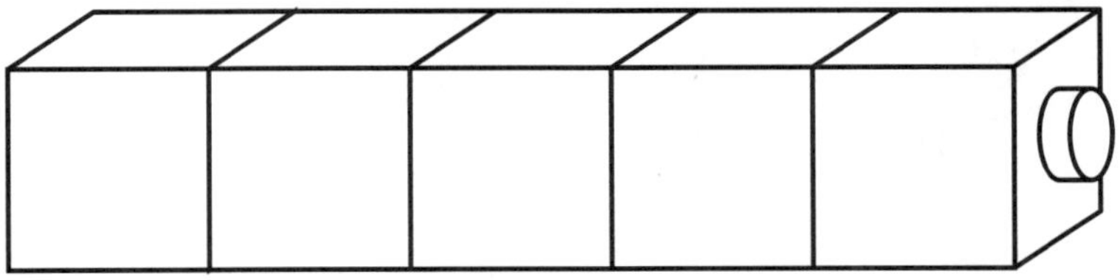

_________ and _________ make 5.

2

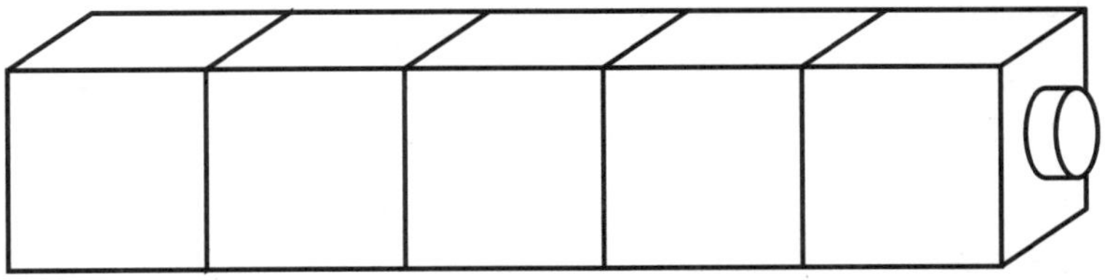

_________ and _________ make 5.

7b Numbers to 5

Color  **red. Color** 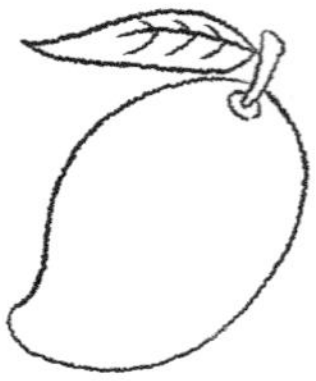 **yellow.**

1

Count. Write.

2 How many  ?

3 How many  ?

4 How many  and  in all?

7c Making Addition Stories

Color 2 ◯ yellow.

Color the rest brown.

1 ◯ ◯ ◯ ◯ ◯

Count. Write.

2 How many ◯ are yellow? ☐

3 How many ◯ are brown? ☐

4 There are ________ ◯ in all.

7d Counting to Add

Count. Write.

1 and 0 make 1.

1

☐ and ☐ make ☐.

2

☐ and ☐ make ☐.

3

☐ and ☐ make ☐.

7e Making Addition Stories

Color some ◯ orange.

Color the rest blue.

1 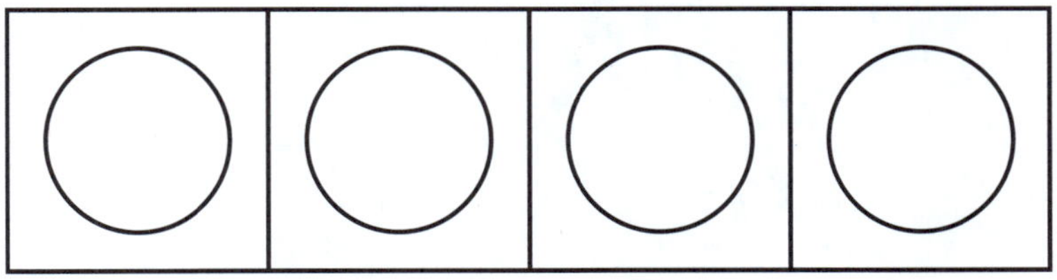

Count. Write.

2 How many ◯ are orange?

3 How many ◯ are blue?

4 There are ________ ◯ in all.

7f Adding

Count. Write.

1

$\square + \square = \square$

2

$\square + \square = \square$

7g Making Addition Stories

Color some ◯ red. Color some ◯ green.

1 ◯ ◯ ◯ ◯ ◯

Count. Write.

2 How many ◯ are red?

3 How many ◯ are green?

Trace.

4 How many ◯ did you color in all?

2 3 4 5

7h Counting to Add

Write.

1. 2 and 1 make ________.

2. 1 and 3 make ________.

3. 3 and 2 make ________.

4. 4 and 1 make ________.

7i Number Facts to 10

Color  **green. Color**  **orange.**

1 

Count. Write.

2 How many  ?

3 How many  ?

4 How many  and  in all?

Fill in each blank.

5 ________ and ________ make ________.

7j Number Facts to 10

Use 2 fruits.
Draw to make 10.

1

Count. Write.

2 ________ and ________ make ________.

7k Counting to Add

Draw ◯ to make 10.

Then, count. Write.

1

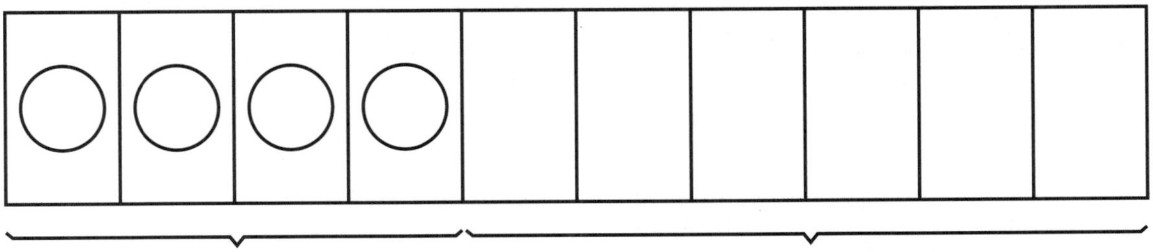

7l Counting to Add

Count. Write.

1

and make .

There are ________  in all.

7m Counting to Add

Match.

1

2 and 3	1 and 2	1 and 1

Count. Write.

2

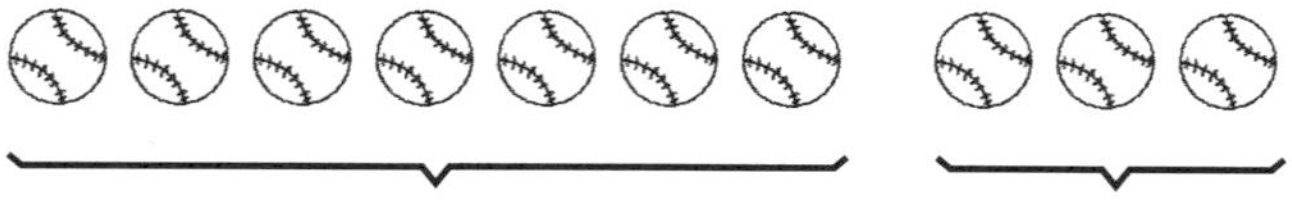

Circle.

3 How many are there in all? **8** **4** **10**

7n Addition Sentences

Color some ◯ yellow. Color the rest green.

1

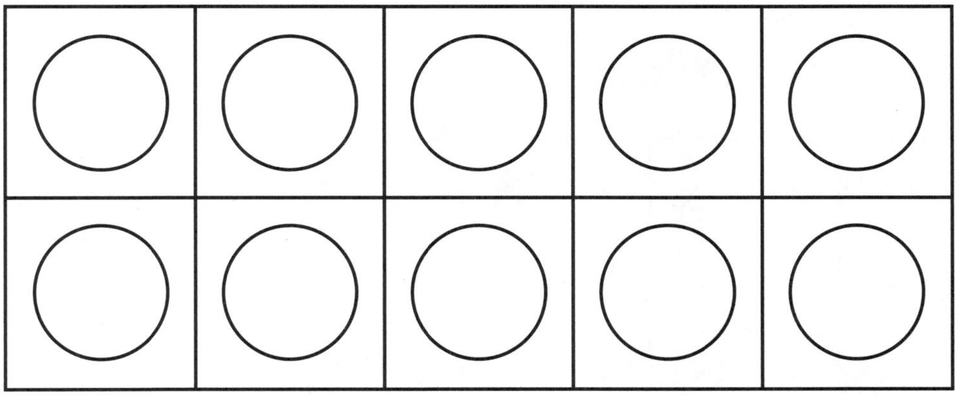

Count. Write.

2 How many ◯ are yellow?

3 How many ◯ are green?

4 ☐ + ☐ = 10

7o Making Addition Stories

Color some ○ red.

Color some ○ yellow.

1 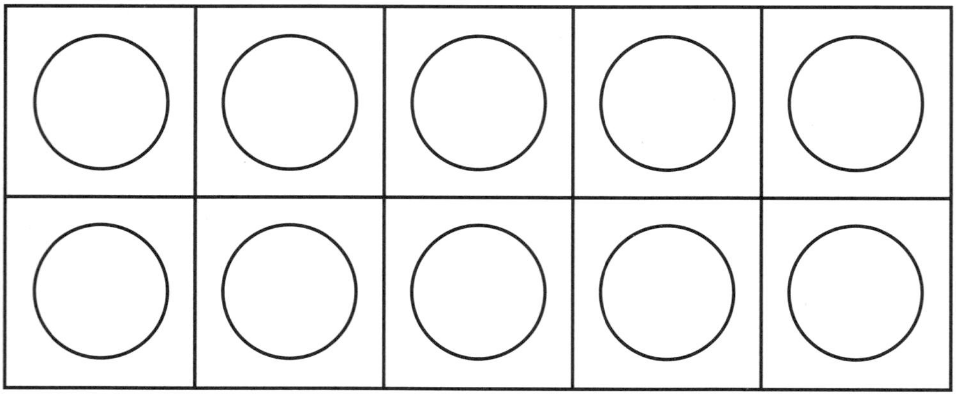

Count. Write.

2 How many ○ are red?

3 How many ○ are yellow?

4 How many ○ did you color in all?

7p Adding

Color the box with the correct number.

1. 1 + 6 =

7
5

2. 2 + 5 =

8
7

3. 4 + 5 =

9
10

4. 7 + 3 =

10
9

5. 6 + 2 =

8
10

BLANK

Name: ______________________ Date: ____________

Chapter 8 Fact Fluency Subtraction

8a Counting to Compare

Count.

Color  **red to show** **.**

1 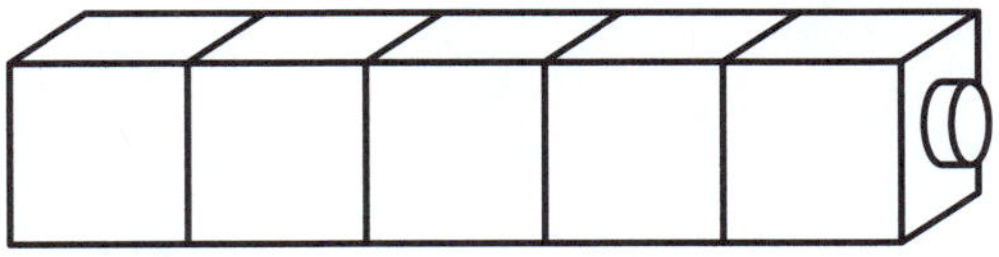

Color  **yellow to show** **.**

2 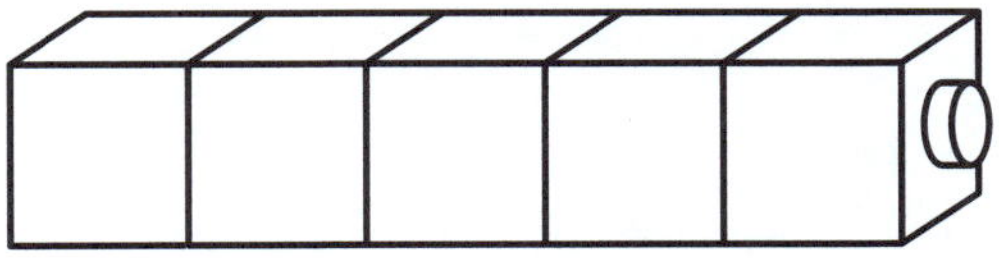

Circle.

3 What is more?  

8b Making Subtraction Stories

Color 3  **red.**

1 

Count. Write.

2 There are ________  in all.

3 ________  are colored red.

4 How many  are **not** red? ☐

8c Number Facts to 5

Use 2 colors to show 5. Count. Write.

1

________ and ________ make ________.

2

________ and ________ make ________.

3

________ and ________ make ________.

8d Subtracting

Make an ✗ to show the subtraction.

Count. Write.

1. 5 − 1

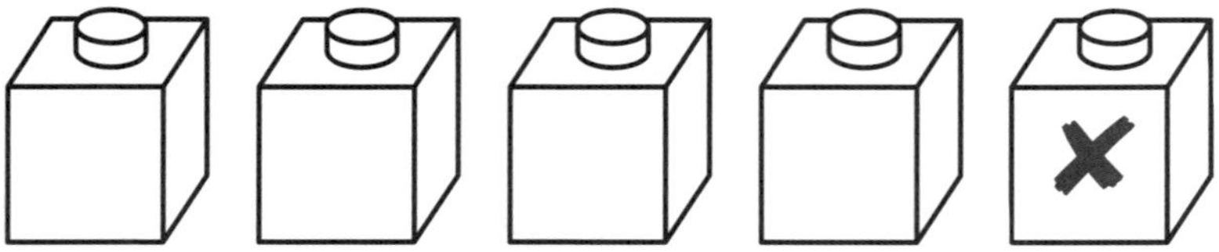

4

2. 4 − 2

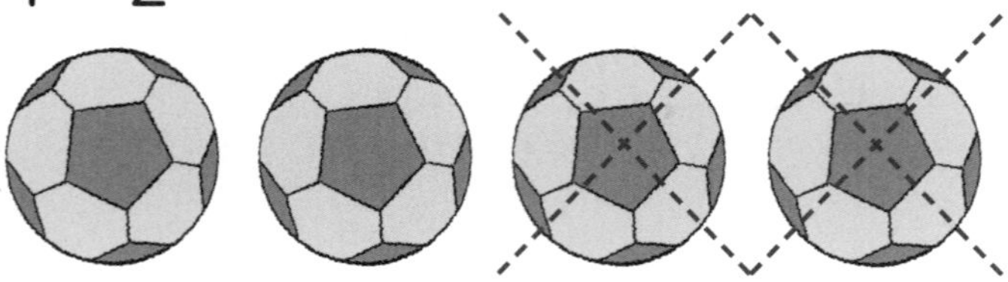

3. 2 − 1

4. 5 − 3

8e Subtracting

Draw a picture to show 5 – 3.

1

Look at your picture.

Count. Write.

2 $5 - 3 =$ ☐

8f Subtracting Within 5

Write. Color to help you.

1. 3 is 1 and ______.

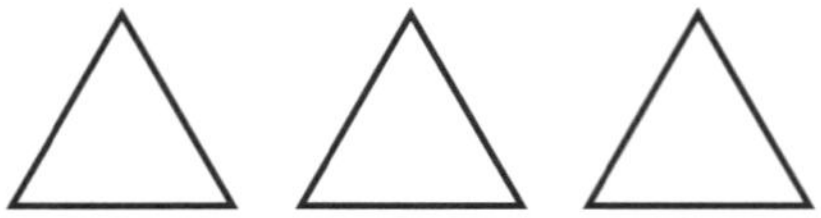

2. 4 is ______ and 3.

3. 4 is 4 and ______.

4. 5 is 1 and ______.

5. 5 is ______ and 3.

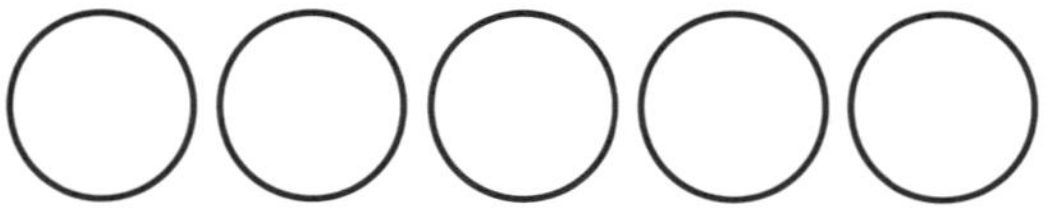

8g Subtracting Within 5

Fill in each blank.

1 How many  and  in all? ☐

2 How many  ? ☐

3 $5 - 3 =$ ☐

There are ________ .

8h Making Subtraction Stories

Color 5  **orange.**

1

Count. Write.

2 There are __________  in all.

3 __________  are colored orange.

4 How many  are **not** orange?

8i Making Subtraction Stories

Count. Write.

1 There are ________ .

2 ________  walk away.

3 There are ________  left.

8j Subtracting

Fill in each blank.

1. How many  and  in all? ☐

2. How many  ? ☐

3. 10 – 6 = ☐

There are ________ .

8k Subtracting

Draw a picture to show 10 – 4.

1

Look at your picture.

Count. Write.

2 10 – 4 = ☐

8I Subtracting

Count. Write.

Which tower has more  ? Circle it.

1

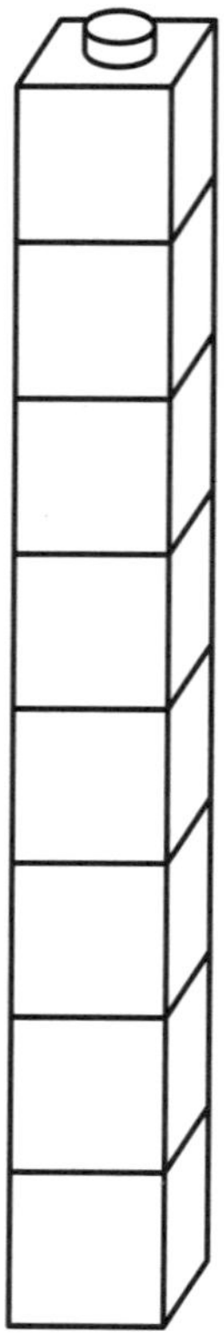

2

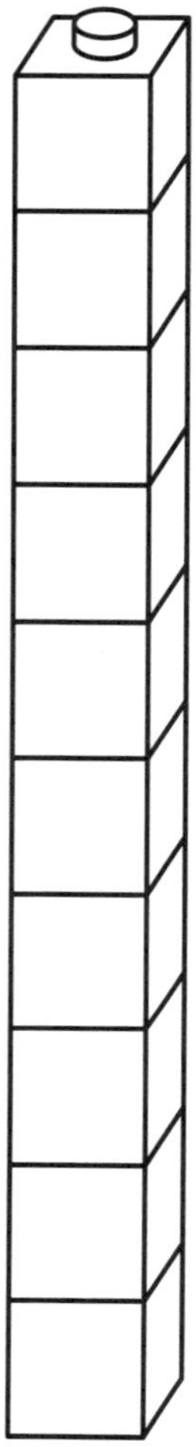

Make an X on  to make both towers the same.

Write.

3 How many  have **X**?

8m Subtracting

Subtract.

1 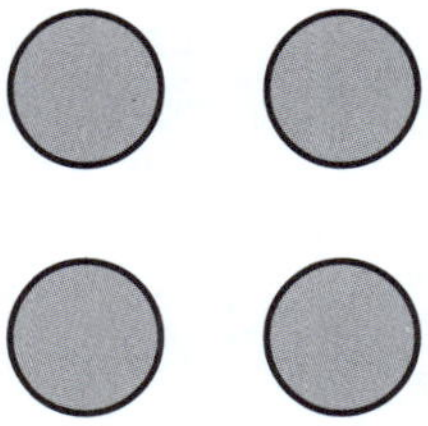 – 2 =

2 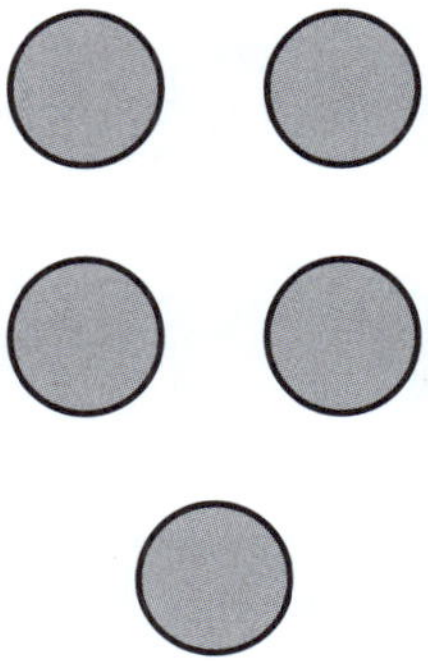 – 4 =

8n Subtracting

Subtract.

1 7 – 2 =

2 8 – 4 =

8o Counting Back to Subtract

Draw on  **.**

Count back to subtract. Write.

1. $7 - 3 =$ ☐

2. $9 - 4 =$ ☐

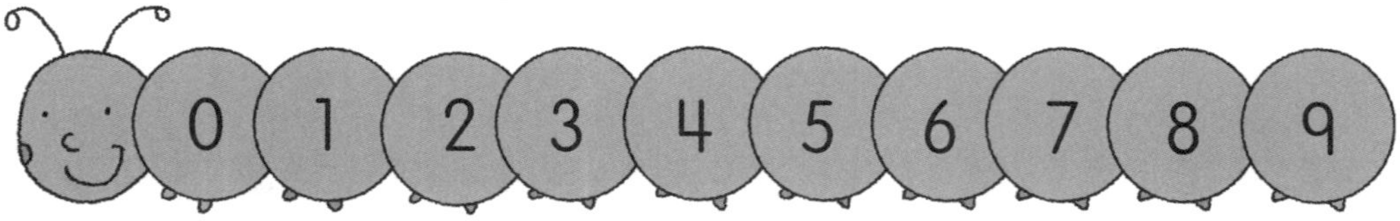

3. $10 - 2 =$ ☐

8p Writing Number Sentence

Color 2  **brown.**

Color 1  **yellow.**

1 

Count. Write.

2 How many  did you color? ☐

---

3 Write a number sentence.

☐ + ☐ = ☐

---

4 How many  did you **not** color? ☐

8q Subtraction Sentences

Jane has 5  . She spends 3  .

Make an ✗ on  to show this.

1 

How many  does she have left?

Fill in each box.

2 ☐ – ☐ = ☐

8r Subtraction Sentences

Choose a number from 5 to 10.

1 My number: ☐

Draw a picture to show your number.

2 ☐

Make an ✗ on 3.

Fill in each box to show this.

3 ☐ − ☐ = ☐

8s Subtraction Sentences

Subtract.

1 $5 - 2 =$ ☐

2 $7 - 4 =$ ☐

Look at the answers above.
Color the correct box.

3 The numbers I get are [the same / different].

Name: ______________________________ Date: ______________

Fact Fluency
Numbers to 100

9a Numbers to 20

Circle group of 10. Count on.
Color the correct number.

1

13
15

2

12
13

3

15
20

9b Numbers to 20

Color 17 ◯.

1

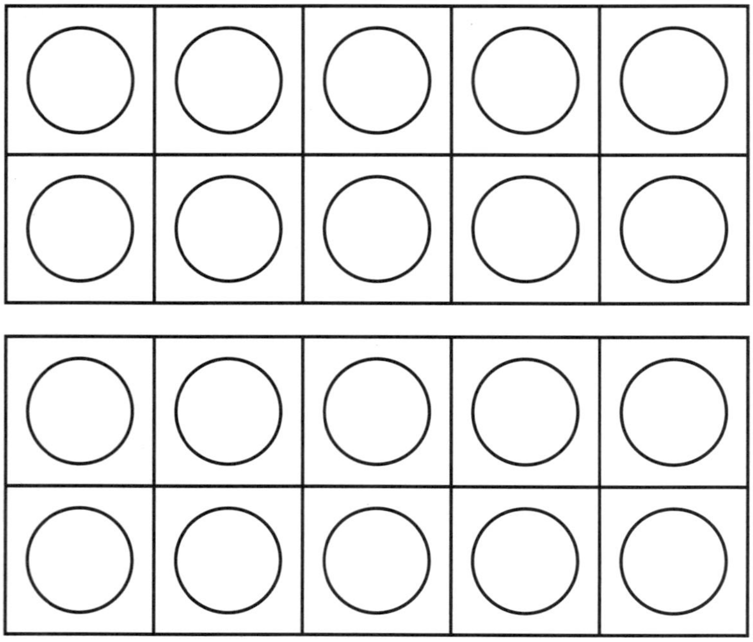

Draw.

2 Show 19.

9c Numbers 21 to 50

Make groups of 10. Color them yellow.
Color the rest purple.

1

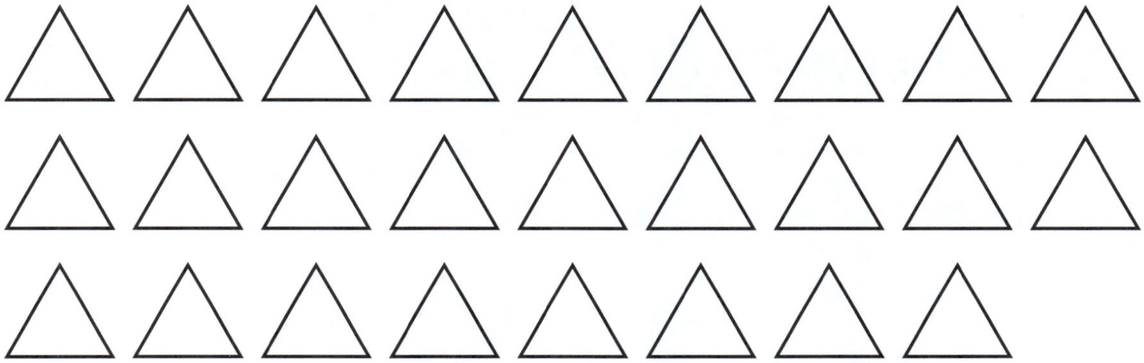

Count. Color.

2 How many △ are yellow?

10
20

3 How many △ are purple?

6
5

4 How many △ are there in all?

16
26

9d Counting On by 10s

Make trains with **.**
Draw.

1 Make 1 train with 10 .

2 Make 2 trains with 10  for each.

Write.
Then, color the box with correct number.

3 How many  did you use in 1?

4 How many  did you use in 2?

5 10, 20, ________.

30	40	60

9e Counting On by 10s

Circle groups of 10.

1 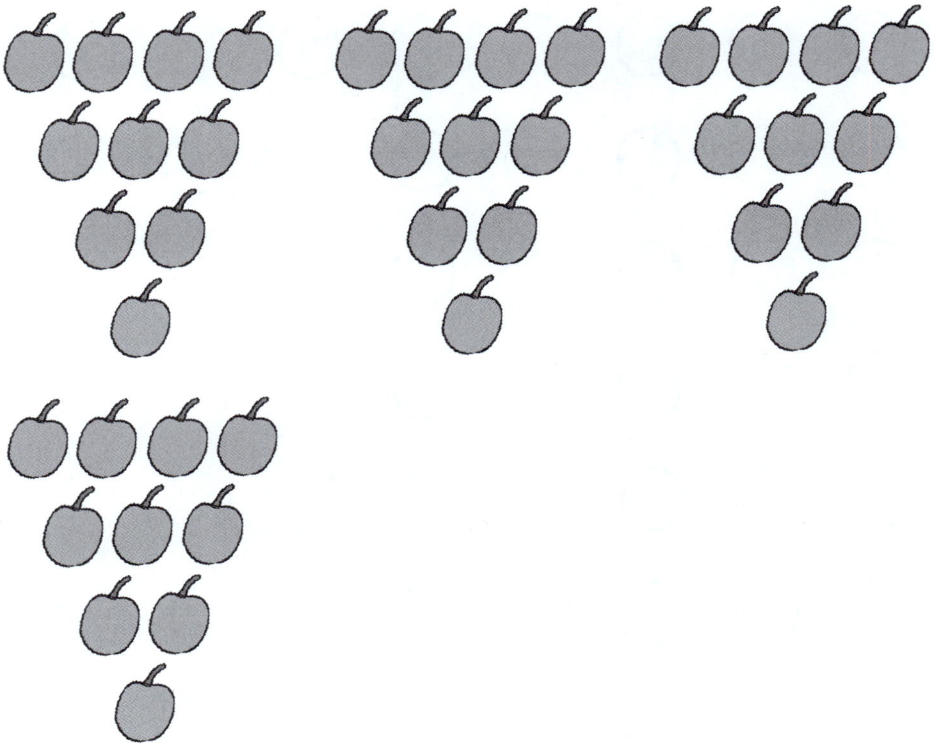

Count. Color.

2 How many groups of  are there?

3
4
5

Count on by 10s. Color.

3 There are

30	40	50

 in all.

9f Numbers 51 to 100

Circle groups of 10. Color the rest purple.

1

Count. Write.

2 How many ◯ are purple? ☐

Circle.

3 How many ◯ are there in all? **51** **56** **61**

9g Numbers 51 to 100

Count on by groups of 10.
Next, count on. Color the box with correct number.

1

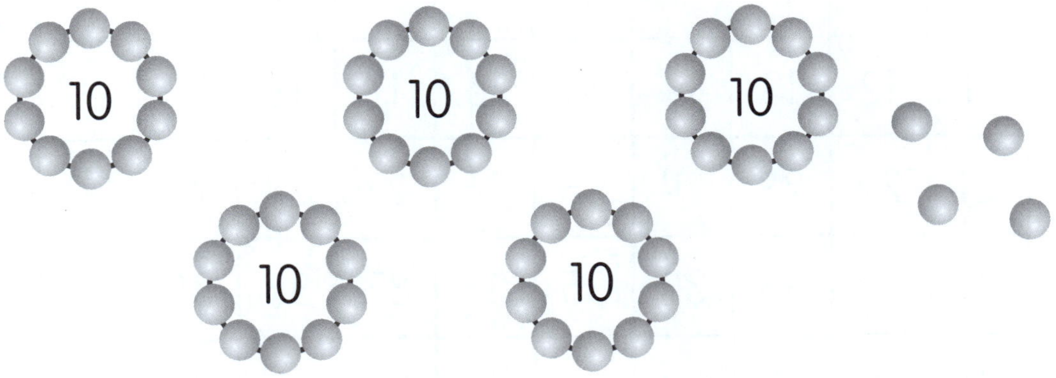

44	54	59

✂ **Cut. Paste to show how you count.**

2 First,

3 Next,

4 Last,

9h Numbers 1 to 100

Color the numbers from 51 to 60.

1

1	2	3	4	5	6	7	8	9	10
11	12	13	14	15	16	17	18	19	20
21	22	23	24	25	26	27	28	29	30
31	32	33	34	35	36	37	38	39	40
41	42	43	44	45	46	47	48	49	50
51	52	53	54	55	56	57	58	59	60
61	62	63	64	65	66	67	68	69	70
71	72	73	74	75	76	77	78	79	80
81	82	83	84	85	86	87	88	89	90
91	92	93	94	95	96	97	98	99	100

Circle numbers on the chart.

2 65

3 72

4 89

9i Counting On and Counting Back

Count on or count back. Color the correct boxes.

1. 11, 12, 13, ?, 15, 16

16	14	13

2. 20, ?, 18, 17, 16, 15

14	17	19

Count on. Write.

3.

11		13	14	

4.

		18	19	

9j Numbers 1 to 100

Use the hundred chart.

1	2	3	4	5	6	7	8	9	10
11	12	13	14	15	16	17	18	19	20
21	22	23	24	25	26	27	28	29	30
31	32	33	34	35	36	37	38	39	40
41	42	43	44	45	46	47	48	49	50
51	52	53	54	55	56	57	58	59	60
61	62	63	64	65	66	67	68	69	70
71	72	73	74	75	76	77	78	79	80
81	82	83	84	85	86	87	88	89	90
91	92	93	94	95	96	97	98	99	100

1. Count on from 81 to 100.

   Move ⬤ along the numbers as you count.

2. Choose a number from 71 to 80.

   Color it green.

9k What is the Number?

1 Choose a number from 1 to 90.

Tell your number to your partner.

Color to show your number.

2

3 Ask your partner to check.

91 More and Less

Count. Color.

1 How many clouds are there?

23
20

Draw clouds to show 1 more.

2

Name: ______________________ Date: ____________

Fact Fluency
Sorting

10a Same and Different

Color 9 ◯ green and 1 ◯ yellow.

1 ◯ ◯ ◯ ◯ ◯
◯ ◯ ◯ ◯ ◯

Color some ◯ orange and some ◯ blue.

2 ◯ ◯ ◯ ◯ ◯
◯ ◯ ◯ ◯ ◯

Tell your partner.

3 How are 1 and 2 same?

4 How are 1 and 2 different?

10b Drawing the Same

1 Draw the same.

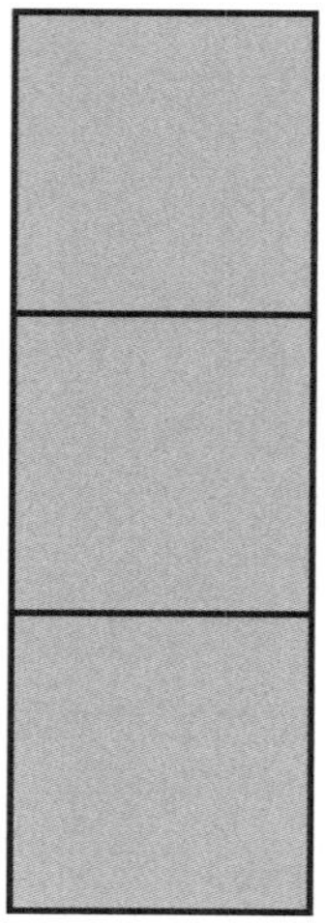

Count. Write.

2 How many  ?

10c Sorting by Color

Color 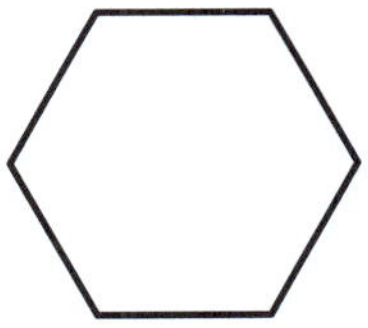 **yellow and**  **red.**

1

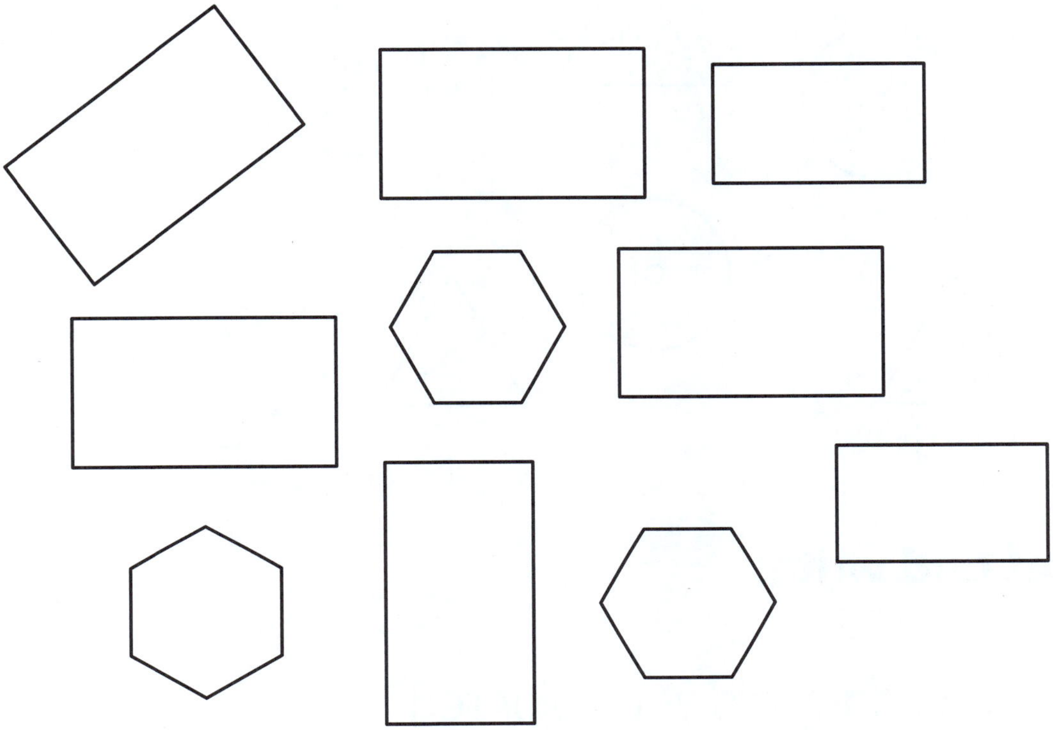

Count. Write.

2 How many are yellow?

3 How many are red?

10d Sorting by Counting

Color shapes with 1 hole red.
Color shapes with 3 holes green.

1

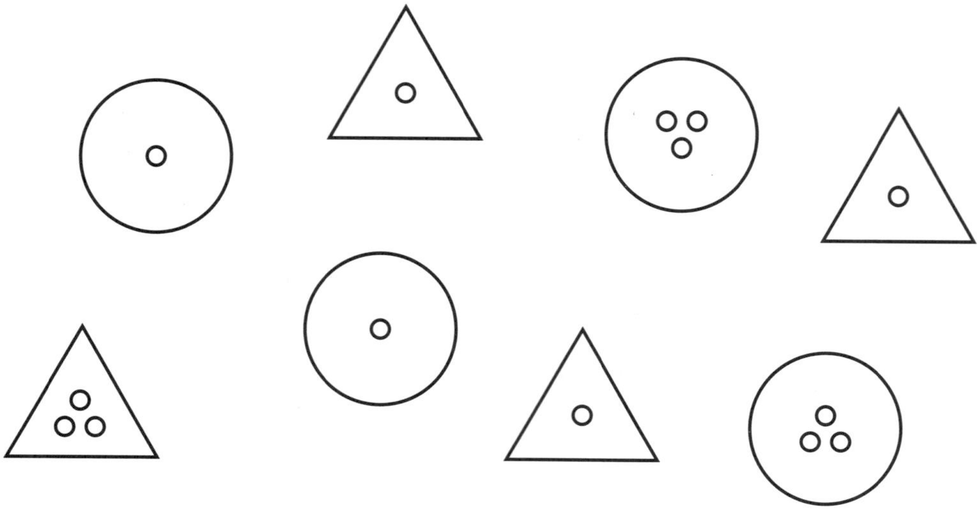

Count and write.

2 How many did you color red?

3 How many did you color green?

10e Sorting by Shapes

Cut. Paste.

1

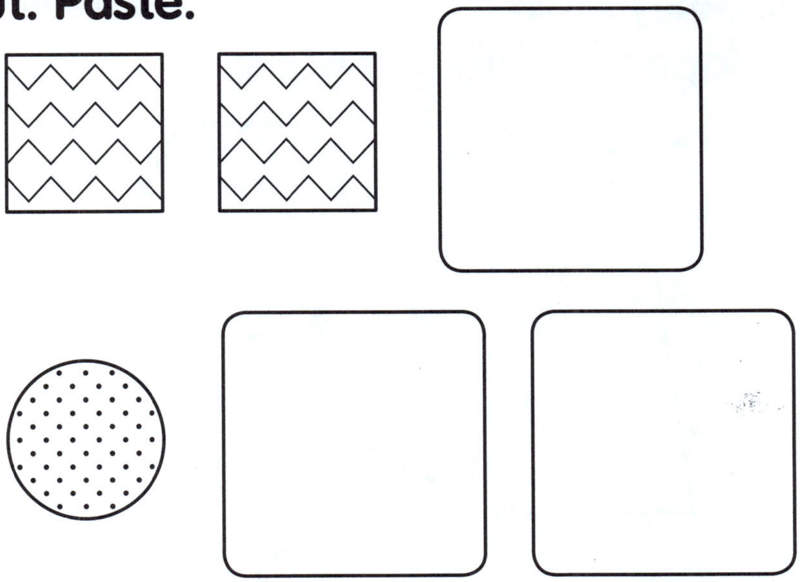

Count. Write.

2 How many  ?

3 How many 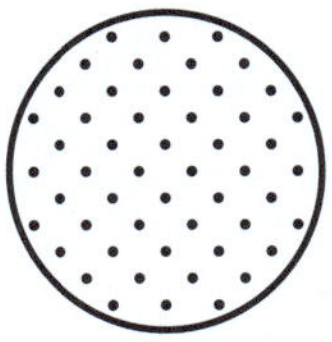 ?

4 How many  and 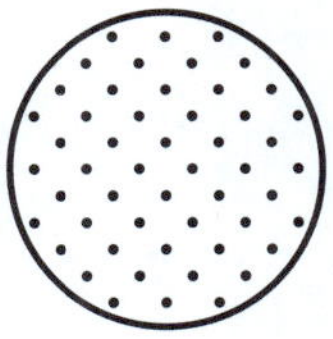 in all?

10f Sorting by Size

Color the big shapes yellow.
Color the small shapes purple.

1

Count. Write.

2 How many are big?

3 How many are small?

10g Same and Different

Draw 3 things that belong together.

1 They have the same shape.

2 They have the same size.

3 They have the same shape and number.

10h Sorting

Draw 3 big shapes and 7 small shapes.

Use ○, △, □, ▭, and ⬡.

1

2 How can you sort these shapes?
Tell your partner about it.

BLANK

1b

1c

1e

1g

3e

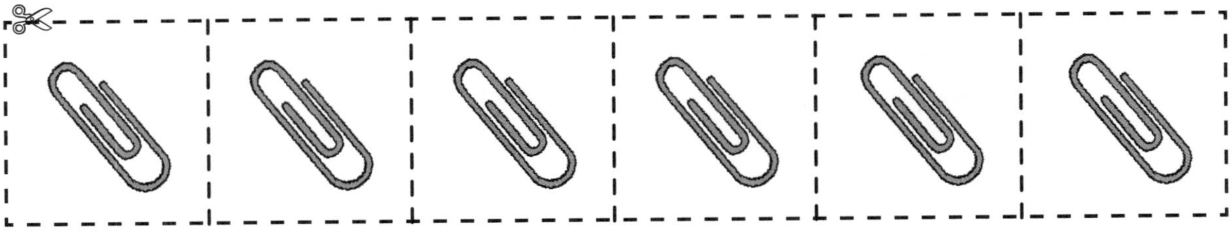

BLANK

4b

9g

I count by 10s to 50.

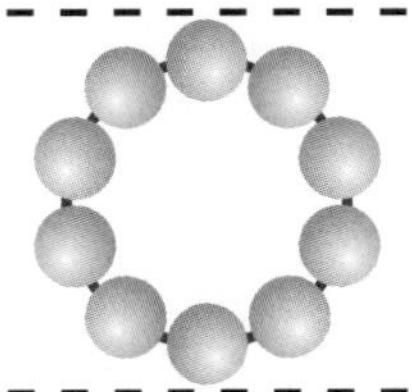

I count on to 54.

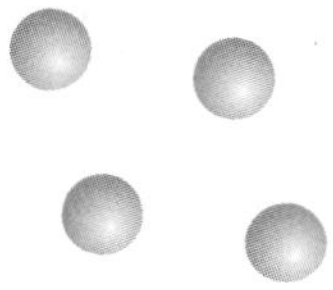

I color my answer.

44	54	59

10e

 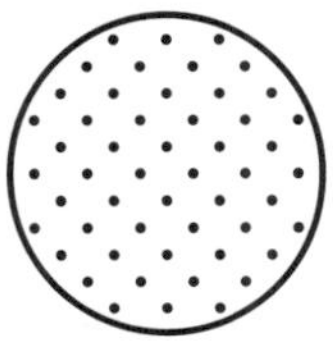 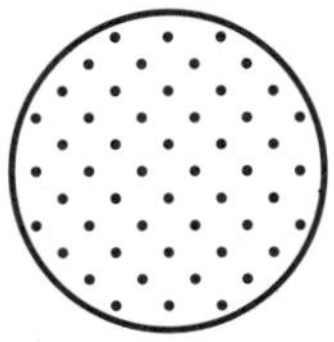

BLANK

Answers

Note:

Instructions to the teacher or parent will appear in italicized type.

Chapter 1

1a *Read the instructions aloud. Give enough wait time for students to do each part of the problem.*

1. Students should color 1 tree.
2. Students should color 2 butterflies.
3. Students should match 1 ball to 1 ball and 2 balls to 2 balls.

1b *Read the instructions aloud. Give enough wait time for students to do each part of the problem.*

1. Students should trace 1; 1; Students should cut and paste the apple.
2. Students should trace 2; Students should color 2 circles.
3. Students should count and trace 1.
4. Students should count and trace 2.

1c

1. Students should color 2 birds.
2. Students should cut and paste to make a set of 2 bears.
3. 1
4. 1
5. 2

1d

1. Students should draw a tower of 3 cubes; Students should trace 3.
2. 1
3. 2
4. 3
5. 3

1e

1. Students should cut and paste to make a set of 4 birds.
2. 2
3. 2
4. Students should trace 4.

1f **Say:** *Draw three ways to show 4 hearts. Have a friend count and say the number.*

1. Answers vary.
2. Answers vary.
3. Answers vary.

1g

1. Students should cut and paste to make a set of 5 fruits.
2. Students should trace 3.
3. Students should trace 5.

1h

1. 2
2. 4
3. 5
4. Students should color the zebras.
5. Students should circle the chickens.

1i *Read the instructions aloud. Encourage students to show 4 and 5 by coloring different squares. Give them enough wait time to color each number.*

1. Students should color 4 squares.
2. Students should color 5 squares.

1j *Read the instructions aloud. Encourage different artistic ways of showing the number chosen.* **Say:** *Choose your favorite number. Then, use pictures or tallies to show the number. Show the number in three different ways.*

1. Answers vary.
2. Answers vary.
3. Answers vary.
4. Answers vary.

1k *Have students point to the word, say, and clap the number. Give them enough wait time to finish each problem.*

1. Answers vary; 1
2. Answers vary; 2
3. Answers vary; 3
4. Answers vary; 4
5. Answers vary; 5

Chapter 2

2a

1. Students should match 1 bead to number 1, 2 beads to number 2, 3 beads to number 3, 4 beads to number 4, and 5 beads to number 5.

2b Students should color 2 groups of 6 worms.

2c

1. 5
2. 1
3. 6

2d

1. Students should trace 6.
2. Students should trace 7.
3. Students should color 7 circles and then write 7.

2e

1. Students should color 4 basketballs orange and 4 beach balls brown.
2. 4
3. 4
4. Students should trace 8.

2f

1. Students should match 5 cubes to number 5, 6 cubes to number 6, 7 cubes to number 7, 8 cubes to number 8, and 9 cubes to number 9.

2g

1. Students should color the whole apples green and the bitten apples red.
2. 5
3. 4
4. Students should trace 9.

2h **Say:** *Think of a number. It can be 6, 7, 8, 9, or 10. Draw something that shows the number in 3 different ways. Then, trade pictures with a partner. Count what you see. Check with your partner's number. Trade pictures again. Tell your partner why you chose your number.*
Answers vary.

2i *Have students point to the word, say, and clap the number.*

1. 7
2. 8
3. 9
4. 10

2j **Say:** *This is a picture of an ocean. Draw 1 to 10 animals that may live in the ocean. Write the number that matches your picture.*
Answers vary. Example: There should be 1 to 10 sea creatures drawn; Answers vary. Example: The number written should match the number of sea creatures drawn.

2k **Say:** *We have to color 2 or 3 cubes. Take out an orange crayon and a purple crayon. You are going to choose how many you color orange or purple. You have to use both colors. At the end of the practice, ask students if their ways to make 2 or 3 will all be the same. Have a discussion about it.*

1. Students should color 1 or 2 cubes orange and color 1 or 2 cubes purple.
2. Accept 1 or 2.
3. Accept 1 or 2.
4. Students should write 2 or 3.

2l

1. 1
2. 3
3. 4

2m

1. 3
2. 2
3. 5
4. 3 ; 2

2n **Say:** *Look at the picture. You can choose what you want to use for your story and the number to show.*
Answers vary.

2o

1. 5
2. 4
3. 9

2p

1. 3
2. 5
3. 8
4. 3 ; 5 ; 8

Chapter 3

3a *If students need more support, have them build trains using math manipulatives and compare.*

1. Students should color the second ribbon.
2. Students should color the train of 5 cubes; 5

3b

1. Students should color the second pencil; 6.
2. Students should color the train of 7 cubes.

3c

1. Students should draw 1 to 8 cubes.
2. Answers vary.

3d

1. 2
2. 3
3. Students should circle the tower of 4 cubes.

3e

1. Students should cut and paste to make sets of 4 paperclips and 2 paperclips; Students should circle the set of 4 paperclips.
2. 6

3f

1. 1; 9
2. Students should circle the side with 1 cube.

   Answers vary. Example: 1 is less than 9, which would make the side with fewer cubes lighter.

3g

1. Students should color the 2-cube tower blue; Students should color the 3-cube tower yellow.
2. 2; 3; 5

3h

1. 9; 9
2. Students should color the same.

3i 5; 4; 5; 4; 9; 9

3j **Say:** *Draw a picture of two cube towers. Each tower can be made up of up to 5 cubes. Ask your partner a question about your towers.*

1. Answers vary.
2. Answers vary.

Chapter 4

4a *Before this practice, ask students to use both their hands to show numbers.* **Say:** *Show me 5. Put up 5 fingers on one hand, and a closed fist of the other. Show me 4. Put up 2 fingers on one hand, and 2 fingers on the other. Ask students if there are other ways to make 4 or 5 with both hands. Continue this type of questioning where you see fit, then allow students to complete the practice.*

1. Answers vary.
2. Answers vary.
3. Answers vary.

4b

1. Students should cut and paste to make a set of 2 strawberries; 2
2. Students should cut and paste to make a set of 3 strawberries; 3
3. Students should cut and paste to make a set of 4 strawberries; 4
4. Students should cut and paste to make a set of 5 strawberries; 5

4c **Say:** *Look at both the groups of objects. Circle the group that has more.*

1. 5; 6; Students should circle the group of bird nests.
2. 7; 8; Students should circle the group of milk buckets.

4d **Say:** *Look at both groups of shapes. Color the group that has fewer.*

1. 5; 4; Students should color the group of apples.
2. 4; 3; Students should color the group of circles.

4e **Say:** *Look at both groups of shapes. Circle the group that has fewer.*

1. 2; 3; Students should circle the group of brooms.
2. 1; 2; Students should circle the mobile phone.

4f **Say:** *Look at the frogs. How many frogs do you count? Look at the lily pads. How many lily pads do you count? How many more lily pads do you need to make the two sets the same amount? (elicit responses) Ask students to draw, to figure out how many more are needed to make the two sets the same amount.*

1. Students should draw 2 lily pads; 2
2. Students should draw 1 mitten; Students should circle 1.
3. Students should draw 2 socks; Students should circle 2.

4g **Say:** *How can you compare the sets in items 1 and 2? Have a discussion about it.*

1. 10
2. 7
3. Students should draw 1, 2, or 3 circles; Accept 1, 2, or 3.

4h **Say:** *How many cubes are in each set? Write your answers. Now, look at the set that has more cubes. Circle the set. Count on from this set to find out how many cubes there are in all.*

1. 5
2. 3

   Students should circle the set of 5 cubes.
3. 8

4i

1. 7
2. 5

   Say: *Circle the set with more cubes. Cross out cubes in the greater set to make both sets the same. How many did you cross out? (elicit responses)*

   Students should circle the set of 7 cubes and cross out 2 cubes in the set.

3. 2

4j

1. 7
2. Students should color 7 squares.

4k

1. Answers vary.
2. 10

4l *Read the instructions aloud if necessary.*

1. 1
2. 4
3. 5
4. 4; 1; 5

4m **Say:** *Think of a number less than 10. It can be 1, 2, 3, 4, 5, 6, 7, 8, or 9. Draw something that shows the number. Then, trade pictures with a partner. Count what you see. Check with your partner's number. Trade pictures again. Tell your partner why you chose your number.*
Answers vary.

Chapter 5

5a

1. 3; 7; 10
2. 4; 6; 10

5b **Say:** *Count the sides.*

1. 4
2. 3

5c **Say:** *Count the flat faces.*

1. 2
2. 1

5d *Read the instructions aloud. Get students ready for this practice with red and orange crayons.* **Ask:** *Which shape is the cone? Which shape is the rectangular prism? How do you know?*

Students should color the 5 cones red; Students should color the 5 rectangular prisms orange.

5e

1. 5
2. 5
3. 10

5f *To put this into context, have students stand up by the chairs at their desks. First, ask them to stand behind the chairs. Next, ask them to pull their chairs out and stand next to their chairs. Then, ask the children to sit.* **Say:** *Look at the picture. Read each question aloud. Allow time for students to write their answers before moving to the next question.*

1. 3
2. 4
3. 7

5g *To put this into context, place a piece of construction paper and a cube on the table. Ask students to put the cube on top of the paper, and then under the paper.* **Say:** *Look at the picture. Read each question aloud. Allow time for students to write their answers before moving to the next question.*

1. 5
2. 4
3. 9

5h

1. 2
2. 3
3. 5

5i *You may want students to look at the triangles and identify the sides of each triangle. Then, start the practice.*

1. 3
2. 6

5j *You may want students to look at the squares and identify the sides of each square. Then, start the practice.*

1. 4
2. 7

5k

1. Students should draw 2 circles.
2. Students should draw a picture with 2 circles, 1 triangle, and 1 square.
3. 4

5l

1. Students should draw a picture with 2 triangles and 1 circle.
2. 3

5m **Say:** *You will draw the same number of shapes in another way. You may choose different shapes to draw.*

1. Answers vary.
2. The number of shapes drawn now must match the number of shapes drawn in item 1.
3. Answers vary.

5n

1. Answers vary.
2. Answers vary.
3. 4

5o 6

5p

1. Students should draw a hexagon.
2. 4
3. 2
4. 6

5q

1. 3
2. 3
3. 6

Chapter 6

6a **Say:** *Count the cubes. Draw what comes next in the pattern. Write the number. What comes after 3? How many cubes should we draw? What number do we write? How do you know?*
Students should draw a tower of 4 cubes;
Students should draw a tower of 5 cubes.

6b 12; 13

6c *Students should write a number from 9 to 12, and draw to match the number. They should then draw to show more than their number. Get them to talk about what they notice.*

1. Answers vary.
2. Answers vary.
3. Answers vary.
4. Answers vary.

6d

1. 12; Students should circle 10 keys.
2. 10
3. 4
4. 4; 14

6e

1. 15
2. Students should draw 6 flowers.
3. 6

6f

1. Students should circle 10 circles.
2. Students should circle 17.

6g

1. 20
2. Students should draw 8 oranges.

6h

1. 9; 11
2. 15
3. 18
4. 17; 14

6i

1. 10
2. 8
3. 18
4. 10; 8; 18

6j

1. 10
2. 9
3. 19

6k *Write the numbers 11 to 20 on the board. Tell students that for this practice, they are working with partners. Ask students to choose a number from the board and then, in Item 1, write the number on their papers. Then, have students trade papers. Ask students to read the number on the page. Then, direct students' attention to Item 2, and ask them to draw a picture that shows the same amount as the number they see on the page. Ask them to talk about why the number and the picture show the same amount. You might want to ask a volunteer to help you model this practice.*

1. Answers vary.
2. Answers vary.

6l **Say:** *Draw circles to show the given number of beach balls.*

1. Students should draw 19 balls and circle 10.
2. 9
3. 19; 10; 9

Chapter 7

7a *Give students two different color crayons to color the sets. Write.*

1. Answers vary. Example:

   Students color 2 cubes in one color; Students color 3 cubes in another color; 2; 3

2. Answers vary. Example:

   Students color 4 cubes in one color; Students color 1 cube in another color; 4; 1

7b *Read the instructions aloud if necessary.*

1. Students should color 3 apples red; Students should color 2 mangoes yellow.
2. 3
3. 2
4. 5

7c

1. Students should color 2 circles yellow and 3 circles brown.
2. 2
3. 3
4. 5

7d *Before this practice, ask students to use both of their hands to show sums.* **Say:** *Show me 1. Put up 1 finger on one hand, and a closed fist of the other. Show me 2. Put up 2 fingers on one hand, and a closed fist on the other. Ask students if there is another way to make 2 with both hands. Continue this type of questioning where you see fit, then allow students to complete the practice.*

1. 1; 1; 2
2. 1; 2; 3
3. 2; 2; 4

7e **Say:** *You have to color all of the circles. Take out an orange crayon and a blue crayon. You are going to choose how many you color orange or blue. You have to use both colors. At the end of the practice, ask students if their ways to make 4 is all the same. Have a discussion about it.*

1. Students should color 1, 2, or 3 circles orange and 3, 2, or 1 circle blue.
2. Accept 1, 2, or 3.
3. Accept 3, 2, or 1.
3. 4

7f

1. 2; 2; 4
2. 3; 2; 5

7g **Say:** *You can color any number of circles. Take out a red crayon and a green crayon. You are going to choose how many you color red or green. You have to use both colors. At the end of the practice, ask students if their ways to make 2, 3, 4, or 5 will all be the same. Have a discussion about it.*

1. Students should color 1, 2, 3, or 4 circles red and color 1, 2, 3, or 4 circles green.
2. Accept 1, 2, 3, or 4.
3. Accept 1, 2, 3, or 4.
4. Students should count the red and green circles and trace 2, 3, 4, or 5.

7h

1. 3
2. 4
3. 5
4. 5

7i *Read the instructions aloud if necessary.*

1. Students should color 6 stalks of broccoli green; Students should color 3 carrots orange.
2. 6
3. 3
4. 9
5. 6; 3; 9

7j

1. Drawings vary.
2. Answers vary; Answers vary; 10

7k Students should draw 6 circles; 4; 6

7l 2; 5; 7; 7

7m *This could be a whole class or an independent practice depending on students' readiness.*

1. Students should match the box with 2 and 3 to 5 hearts, box with 1 and 2 to 3 stars, and box with 1 and 1 to 2 smiley faces.
2. 7; 3
3. Students should circle 10.

7n **Say:** *You have to color all of the circles. Take out a yellow crayon and a green crayon. You are going to choose how many you color yellow or green. You have to use both colors. At the end of the practice, ask students if their ways to make 10 is all the same. Have a discussion about it.*

1. Answers vary.
2. Answers vary.
3. Answers vary.
4. Answers vary; Answers vary

7o **Say:** *You can color any number of circles. Take out a red crayon and a yellow crayon. You are going to choose how many you color red or yellow. You have to use both colors. At the end of the practice, ask students if their ways to make 2, 3, 4, 5, 6, 7, 8, 9, or 10 is all the same. Have a discussion about it.*

1. Answers vary.
2. Answers vary.
3. Answers vary.
4. Answers vary.

7p

1. Students should color 7.
2. Students should color 7.
3. Students should color 9.
4. Students should color 10.
5. Students should color 8.

Chapter 8

8a

1. Students should color 3 cubes.
2. Students should color 2 cubes.
3. Students should circle the apple.

8b

1. Students should color 3 hearts red.
2. 5

3 3

4 2

8c *Prepare students for this practice with 2 crayons.* **Say:** *What are the different ways to make 5? (elicit responses)*

1 Answers vary; Answers vary; 5

2 Answers vary; Answers vary; 5

3 Answers vary; Answers vary; 5

8d **Say:** *Cross out to subtract. How many are left? Write the number.*

1 Students should trace 4.

2 Students should cross out 2 soccer balls; 2

3 Students should cross out 1 tricycle; 1

4 Students should cross out 3 marbles; 2

8e **Say:** *Draw a picture to show 5. Cross out to show what you are subtracting.*

1 Drawings vary.

2 2

8f

1 2

2 1

3 0

4 4

5 2

8g *Read aloud the instructions and questions if necessary.*

1 5

2 3

3 2; 2

8h

1 Students should color 5 hearts orange.

2 7

3 5

4 2

8i

1 9

2 5

3 4

8j

1 10

2 6

3 4; 4

8k **Say:** *Draw a picture to show 10. Cross out to show what you are subtracting.*

1 Drawings vary.

2 6

8l **Say:** *Circle the set with more cubes. Cross out cubes in the greater set to make both sets the same. How many did you cross out?*

1 8

2 10
Students should circle the set of 10 cubes and cross out 2 cubes in the set.

3 2

8m

1 2

2 1

8n

1 5

2 4

8o **Say:** *Count back to show the subtraction. What number do you start with? How many times do you count back? (elicit responses)*

1 4

2 5

3 8

8p **Say:** *How many bows did you color brown? How many bows did you color yellow? How many bows did you color in all? (elicit responses) Encourage student to show this as an addition sentence.*

1. Students should color 2 bows brown and 1 bow yellow.
2. 3
3. 2; 1; 3
4. 2

8q *Read the instructions aloud.*

1. Students should cross out 3 coins.
2. 5; 3; 2

8r *This can be used as a partner practice. Ask students to choose a number and draw.*

1. Answers vary.
2. Answers vary.

   Students should cross out 3 objects in their pictures.
3. Answers vary; 3; Answers vary

8s

1. 3
2. 3
3. Students should color the same.

Chapter 9

9a *Ask students to look for groups of 10 and count on from 10*

1. Students should color 15.
2. Students should color 12.
3. Students should color 20.

9b

1. Students should color 17 circles.
2. Drawings vary.
   Ask students to make a 10 to show the counting in their drawings.

9c *Prepare students for this practice with a yellow and a purple crayon.* **Say:** *How many 10s do you see? Have a discussion. Color groups of 10 in yellow. You may want to do this practice with the whole class. Stress that you are looking at the groups of 10. Then, focus on the triangles left, and color them purple. Finally, have students count how many triangles are there in all.*

1. Students should color 2 groups of 10 triangles yellow; Students should color 6 triangles purple.
2. Students should color 20.
3. Students should color 6.
4. Students should color 26.

9d

1. Students should draw a train of 10 cubes.
2. Students should draw 2 trains of 10 cubes each.
3. 10
4. 20
5. Students should color 30.

9e **Say:** *What do you count by? Tell your partner how you know.*

1. Students should circle 4 groups of 10 apples.
2. Students should color 4.
3. Students should color 40.

9f *Prepare students for this practice with a purple crayon.* **Say:** *How many 10s do you see? Circle them. Then, color the circles left.*

1. Students should circle 6 groups of 10 circles. Students should color 1 circle purple.
2. 1
3. Students should circle 61.

9g

1. Students should color 54.
2. I count by 10s to 50.
3. I count on to 54.
4. I color my answer.

9h *Ask students to look at the hundred chart. As you read the numbers with the class, have them say the numbers with you.*

1. Students should color the numbers from 51 to 60.
2. Students should circle 65.
3. Students should circle 72.
4. Students should circle 89.

9i

1. Students should color 14.
2. Students should color 19.
3. 12; 15
4. 16; 17; 20

9j *Ask students to look at the hundred chart.* **Say:** *How is this chart different than the one you have seen before? (elicit responses)*

1. Students should move the counter as they count from 81 to 100.
2. Students should choose any number from 71 to 80 and color it green.
   Answers vary.

9k *This is a partner practice that requires them to use the number cubes to count on by tens and ones. Read the instructions aloud if necessary.*

1. Answers vary.
2. Answers vary.
3. Answers vary.

9l *Read the instructions aloud and give students time to count and write the number and then draw 1 more.*

1. Students should color 23.
2. Students should draw to show 24.

Chapter 10

10a

1. Students should color 9 circles green;
   Students should color 1 circle yellow.
2. Students should color some circles orange;
   Students should color some circles blue.
3. Answers vary. Example: The number of circles in all is 10.
4. Answers vary. Example: I use different colors for different number of circles.

10b

1. Students should draw a tower of 3 cubes.
2. 3

10c **Say:** *Look at the shapes. What shapes do you see? (elicit responses) The question asks how many shapes of each color are there. Do you see rectangles? Do you see hexagons? (elicit responses)*

1. Students should color 3 hexagons yellow;
   Students should color 7 rectangles red.
2. 3
3. 7

10d **Say:** *Look at the shapes. What shapes do you see? (elicit responses) The question asks for shapes with different number of holes. Which shapes can you color red? Which shapes can you color green? (elicit responses)*

1. Students should color 3 triangles and 2 circles with 1 hole each red; Students should color 1 triangle and 2 circles with 3 holes each green.
2. 5
3. 3

10e

1. Students should cut and paste a square;
   Students should cut and paste 2 circles.
2. 3
3. 3
4. 6

10f **Say:** *Color the big shapes yellow. Color the small shapes purple.*

1. Students should color 5 big shapes yellow;
   Students should color 5 small shapes purple.
2. 5
3. 5

10g **Say:** *Look around you. What shapes can you see? (elicit responses) Which 3 things have the same shape? (elicit responses) Which things are about the same in size? (elicit responses) Which things have the same shape and are in the same amount? (elicit responses)*

1. Answers vary.
2. Answers vary.
3. Answers vary.

10h **Say:** *The question asks you to draw big and small shapes. You may choose to draw different shapes like circles, triangles, squares, rectangles, and hexagons for each big and small shapes. For example, you can draw a big triangle as one of the big shapes and a small triangle as one of the small shapes. Choose 2 crayons to color your shapes. What do you observe? Have a discussion about it.*

1. Answers vary.
2. Answers vary.